D1557805

The
Concise History
of
Islam

and the
Origin of its Empires

Gregory C. Kozlowski

Introduction
by
H. D. S. Greenway

Copley Publishing Group
Acton, Massachusetts 01720

Printed in the United States of America

ISBN 0-87411-489-6

10 9 8 7 6 5 4 3 2 1

BP
161.2
.K68
1991

Library of Congress Cataloging-in-Publication Data

Kozlowski, Gregory C.
    The concise history of Islam and the origin of its
empires/Gregory C. Kozlowski.
        p.   cm.
    Includes bibliographic references.
    ISBN 0-87411-489-6
    1. Islam.   2. Civilization, Islamic.   I. Title.
BP161.2.K68   1991
297' .09--dc20
                                                    91-15518
                                                    CIP

CONTENTS

Maps

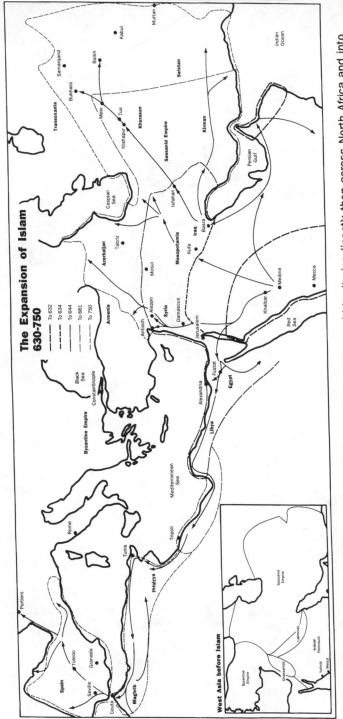

The Expansion of Islam 630-750

- - - - - To 632
- - - - - To 634
——— To 644
- · - · - To 661
- - - - - To 750

Byzantine Empire

Sassanid Empire

Samarqand · Balkh · Kabul · Multan

Transoxania

Bukhara ·

Merv · Tus

Nishapur · **Khurasan**

Selstan

Kirman

Caspian Sea

Istafan

Persian Gulf

Indian Ocean

Azerbaijan

Tabriz ·

Mosul ·

Mesopotamia

Kufa · **Iraq** Basra

Medina ·

· Mecca

Armenia

Antioch · Aleppo ·

Syria Damascus ·

Jerusalem ·

Khaibar ·

Red Sea

Black Sea

Constantinople

Byzantine Empire

Rome ·

Mediterranean Sea

Tripoli

Fustat

Alexandria

Egypt

Libya

Ifriqiya

Tunis ·

Maghrib

Ceuta

Portiers ·

Toledo ·

Granada · Seville ·

Spain

West Asia before Islam

Byzantine Empire

Sassanid Empire

Ghassanids

Lakhmids

Arabian Peninsula

Yathrib ·

Mecca ·

Islam spread rapidly from the Arabian Peninsula into Byzantine and Sassanid territories (inset); then across North Africa and into Spain in the west, and to the Indus and Syr Darya in the east.

vi

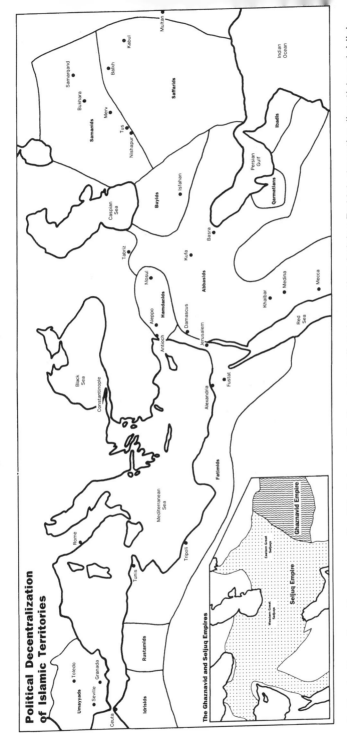

Political Decentralization of Islamic Territories

By the tenth century, the process of political decentralization was well underway, thus helping Turkish dynasties (inset) to establish their rule in succeeding centuries.

vii

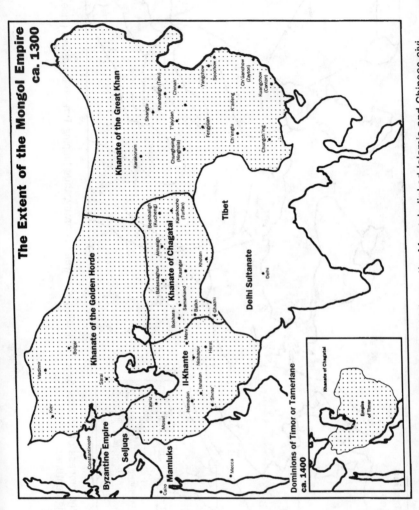

The Extent of the Mongol Empire ca. 1300

Using the Eurasian Steppe as a highway, the Mongols linked Islamic and Chinese civi-

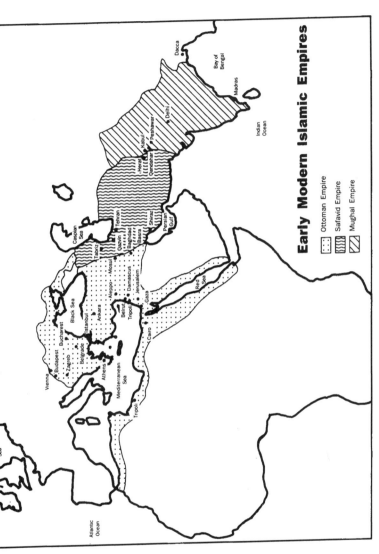

Early Modern Islamic Empires

- Ottoman Empire
- Safavid Empire
- Mughal Empire

By the mid-sixteenth century, Ottoman expansion into Europe had reached the outskirts of Vienna, and the Safavids had in large part defined the boundaries of modern Iran; by the mid-seventeenth century, Mughal rule would extend to almost the southernmost tip of South Asia.

Introduction

American hostages chained to radiators in damp Beirut cellars, the noble Bedouin in his desert fastness, Lawrence of Arabia, "The Desert Song," the storied Baghdad of "A Thousand and One Arabian Nights" and the brutal Baghdad of Saddam Hussein are conflicting images of the Islamic world that have attracted and repelled the West for more than a thousand years.

The story of Islamic civilization is a story as fresh as the morning headlines and as old as Medieval legend, a religious tradition and culture that claims the allegiance of one fifth of the world's population, stretching from the Atlantic to the Philippine Sea.

On one level Islam has been in conflict with Christendom since the eighth century, when Charles Martel turned back an Arab army in France. For the better part of 500 years, starting with the First Crusade to capture the holy places of Jerusalem in 1099 to the successful defense of Malta by the Knights of St John against the Turks in 1565, Christian Europe and the Islamic Orient—the Cross and the Crescent moon—were locked in mortal combat. More recently, Islamic countries and the Jewish state have been at war, but Jerusalem remains at the center of the struggle.

There is a millennium of folk memory dividing the West from the Islamic world that hinders our understanding and appreciation of a major religion and value system with a history and culture that has enriched the world.

In this small book, Gregory C. Kozlowski gives us a traveller's guide to Islamic history that is an invaluable aid to our understanding of a world so often misunderstood. In less than 100 pages, Kozlowski explains the origins of the Islamic religion and its glorious Caliphates and Empires of the Golden Age. He explains the historic, 1200 year old split between Shiite Muslims and Sunni Muslims, whose enmity still continues in Iraq, the country where the schism began.

It was an age in which literature, art and science flourished while Western culture descended into the dark ages. Much of Western culture was kept alive in the libraries of the Islamic world after the collapse of Rome, and the empires of the East far outshone anything in the West until the seventeenth and eighteenth centuries.

There are also important chapters on the holy book, the *Koran*, as well as chapters on Islam as a political system and as a "civilizational system." This is invaluable for understanding a set of values in which there is technically no separation of church and state.

Besides the hard, historic facts, Kozlowski gives us a taste of Islamic legends and poetry as well. For the twelfth century Rubaiyat of Omar Khayyam and the teachings of the Ayatollah Khomeini are both inseparable products of Islam and the Persian past.

H. D. S. Greenway
Boston, Massachusetts
April, 1991

The
Concise History
of
Islam
and the Origin of its Empires

I
The Eve of Muslim Conquest

In the seventh century A.D., civilization was very old in West Asia. Some cities, like Damascus and Aleppo, had their origins in the earliest periods of urban life. Many other cities dated from the days of Alexander's conquests or the Roman empire. These cities were important centers of trade and manufacture. Intellectuals and religious leaders made their homes in the cities of West Asia. While the worship of the old gods continued to be influential in the countryside, the many forms of Christianity and Judaism became dominant in the cities. Representatives of the Churches of Antioch, Jerusalem, Damascus, Constantinople, and Alexandria took the lead in the theological debates and councils.

These cities also preserved the remnants of Hellenistic cultural life. Though *gymnasions* had for some time been transformed into synagogues and catechistic schools, the cities still tried to provide citizens with a primary education. Advanced study in philosophy, theology, rhetoric, and medicine was carried on on a private basis. Individual teachers instructed a few students, often their own children or the sons of relatives and friends, in those specialized topics.

Hellenistic inspiration The ravages of time have all but obliterated the record of life in the cities of the Iranian plateau and Mesopotamia. Like the cities of Palestine, Egypt, and Syria, they had experienced the influence of Hellenism. The ruins of Persian cities from the period showed that Hellenistic architecture inspired the vision of Persian builders. If the character of Persian buildings displayed the impact of Alexander's conquests, then perhaps life in the cities of the Persian Empire also reflected patterns of thought

1

and behavior similar to those of the cities located farther west. Christians and Jews were well represented in the cities of the Sassanid Empire. Zoroastrianism, the Old Persian religion, was apparently practiced only at the imperial court and in a few such isolated areas as the province of Pars. Because of the scattered distribution of towns and villages in the region, the preservation of Persian culture depended on the local land-controllers (*dehqans*). These chiefs provided "knights" for the Sassanid armies and preserved much of the pre-Islamic culture, including the legends surrounding Alexander's life.

Politically, West Asia was divided by the competing superpowers of the day: the Sassanid Empire and the Eastern Roman Empire, known to moderns as the Byzantine Empire. The impasse occurred when the Romans tried to follow in the footsteps of Alexander the Great. First they came up against the empire of the Parthians, an Indo-Aryan group from the steppe who moved on to the Iranian plateau about 250 B.C. In 53 B.C., the Parthians defeated a Roman army at Carrhae. They continued to hold off the Romans until the Parthian Empire fell about A.D. 233. The Sassanids arose to take over where the Parthians left off.

As the eastern capital of the Roman Empire, Constantinople, became the center of authority for the Romans in West Asia, the Sassanids took up the struggle with it. In the midst of this long war, which weakened both Sassanids and Romans, no one paid much attention to the speakers of the Arabic language scattered throughout the area. They seemed to be an odd collection of nomadic tribes, merchants, and peasants. Occasionally either the Byzantines or the Sassanids would support one or another Arab king in the hope of turning him into a buffer on their mutual frontier. Both recruited Arabs for their armies, but the leaders of the major states did not consider these people to be either a major threat or an important

2

asset. However, the Arabian Peninsula was, in the sixth and seventh centuries A.D., nurturing a force of Arabs who eventually would sweep away the Sassanids and bring the Byzantines to the verge of collapse.

The Arabian Peninsula

Located at the edge of the Fertile Crescent, the Arabian Peninsula always played an important role in the histories of the nearby regions. As the home of the Prophet Muhammad and the site of Islam's holiest shrine, it eventually came to have influence in the world beyond West Asia.

Except for Yemen, its southwestern tip, the peninsula itself has always been a barren place. Underground rivers and springs sometimes provided sufficient supplies of water to sustain agricultural oases or towns based on trade. Because of its lack of water and fertile land, the peninsula was the constant source of migrants and invaders who found their way to the richer portions of West Asia. Just as the Central Asian steppe provided the breeding ground for wave after wave of the pastoral nomads who entered the Iranian plateau to the west and China to the east, the Arabian Peninsula was the original home for those who moved into, and sometimes conquered, Egypt, Syria, or the land between the rivers.

The Arab People

Euro-Americans tend to identify the faith of Islam completely with the desert nomads (Bedouin) of the Arabian Peninsula and solely with the Prophet Muhammad. While the second proposition is incorrect from the perspective of Muslim belief, the former is false historically. Let us begin with a more comprehensive account of the ways in which Arabs

3

lived at the time of the Prophet Muhammad's birth (A.D. 570).

Merchants Trade between the Mediterranean littoral and India was centuries old. Ships carried goods through the Indian Ocean and up the Red Sea. An early version of the Suez Canal provided, via the Nile, a direct link with the Mediterranean Sea. Other ships used the Persian Gulf, unloading their cargoes in Iran or Iraq, from where the goods went over land to the markets of Anatolia and Syria. Several caravan routes also carried the products of India and China into West Asia. The most famous was the "Silk Road," which originated in China, traversed the Gobi Desert and the Central Asian steppe, joining in eastern Iran the roads used by caravans from India. After leaving Khorasan, the easternmost province of the Persian Empire, the merchants moved west across the Iranian plateau until they reached the Mediterranean.

Beginning in the fourth century A.D., a major disruption occurred in these established commercial relations. The old Suez Canal silted up, eventually disappearing completely. More importantly, the ongoing conflict between the Byzantine and Sassanid empires led to the closing of the Persian Gulf and the Silk Road to goods intended for Byzantium. To meet a continuing Byzantine demand for the products of China and India, a new commercial avenue opened up. Merchants began to bring their cargoes to the western coast of the Arabian Peninsula. From there, Arab traders hauled the goods by donkey and camel caravan across the peninsula, through Palestine, and into Byzantine Syria or to the Mediterranean's ports. Before that significant alteration in international trade, the Arabian Peninsula had been largely isolated from incursions by foreigners.

Outside of the agricultural produce of the Yemen, the Arabian Peninsula supplied a few aromatic tree resins: frankincense and myrrh, which were used in

4

embalming and in making incense, the ancient world's version of air freshener. On the agricultural oases of the upper peninsula, farmers mostly exported dried dates, a staple food providing, for example, portable rations for travelers or merchants.

With the establishment of the peninsular caravan route, new cities sprang up in areas that were otherwise empty. *Mecca* (more correctly, *Makkah*) was one of the cities that owed its existence to the influx of commercial wealth. In Mecca, a core of wealthy merchant families came to dominate the city's social and political order. Mecca's merchants also developed extensive trade networks by sending branches of their families to settle in the cities of Syria and Palestine. A particularly strong connection arose between Mecca and Damascus.

In order to ensure the safe passage of their caravans through the peninsula, the traders of Mecca created an elaborate series of alliances with the Bedouin whose territories they crossed. Religion formed one of the bonds linking these nomads to the city of Mecca. In the city itself, the Kaabah (literally, "the cube"), a shrine that tradition held the Prophet Abraham (in Arabic, Ibrahim) had built, served as a center for this aspect of the Meccan treaty system. The Meccans encouraged allied Bedouin to bring their sacred objects into the Kaabah. Those who were Christians brought in religious paintings such as pictures of Mary and Jesus. Others who worshiped rocks or oddly-shaped tree branches brought them. By guarding the Kaabah and its precious religious symbols, the Meccans also developed a thriving pilgrimage trade.

The Prophet Muhammad was born into a family that had a prominent role in creating Mecca's commercial empire. Muhammad's great-grandfather, Hashim, was one of the major architects of the system of alliances that was the foundation of Meccan prosperity. Since the Prophet and most of his early followers were merchants, the influence of urban life and commercial activity was strong on the first Muslims, much stronger than that derived from the desert tribes.

Arabs as agriculturalists At the time of the Prophet's birth, many of the people who spoke Arabic were settled on the agricultural oases of the Peninsula. Yathrib, the city in which the Prophet lived for the last ten years of his life, was on one of these. In addition, for several hundred years Arabic-speaking peasants had been settling in those areas of Iraq, Syria, Palestine, and the Iranian plateau that bordered the Arabian Peninsula.

These settled populations formed the basis for two Arab kingdoms, that of the Ghassanids and that of the Lakhmids. Though their kings traced their ancestry to tribes that migrated from the southern portion of the Arabian Peninsula, by the fifth century A.D., both the Ghassanid and Lakhmid kingdoms were based on communities of settled Arab farmers. The kings of both dynasties sponsored sophisticated court cultures. They supervised the writing of the Arabic language in a script adapted from a people called the Nabataeans. The script was the basis for a distinctive Arabic form of writing, which emerged after the death of the Prophet.

In the sixth century A.D., the Byzantines and Sassanids tried to use the kingdoms of Ghassan and Lakhm as frontier posts in their centuries-long war. The constant round of attack and counter attack eventually wore down both states. The continuing influence of the Ghassanids and Lakhmids was felt primarily in the Arabic language. The kings of these dynasties were great patrons of Arabic poets. They believed that the Arabic spoken by the Bedouins was the purest form of the language and that their poetry was the best, so they were the first to make collections of poetry written before the time of the Prophet.

Arabs as nomads: Bedouin In the seventh century A.D., nomadic Arabs were probably a minority among the speakers of that language. They lived, as pastoralists usually do, at the thin edge between civilized societies and lands totally devoid of humans. They were poor and dependent upon the cities for many of the necessities of life such as metal tools, weapons, pots for storage, and kettles for cooking.

The nomadic groups did, however, provide a source of manpower, which could be mobilized for war. While the merchants of Mecca or the farmers of Yathrib had only limited experience in using the sword, lance, and bow, the nomads had to hunt for food with the last and fend off their enemies with the first two. Since nomadic Arabs sometimes raided settled communities or brawled with their neighbors over the use of waterholes and pastures, they had an elementary understanding of how to organize attacks, retreats, feints, and the other tactics of battle. The poverty of nomadic life had few attractions, so when the Arab Empire began its conquest of Syria, Egypt, Iraq, and Iran following the death of the Prophet, the nomads flocked to join the armies. This resulted in the scattering of the desert tribes throughout the empire. Eventually most of them settled down in the cities or became farmers so that the Bedouin became a tiny minority among the Arabs.

The idea that the Prophet Muhammad was a Bedouin, that his preaching was directed primarily at the "passionate sons of the desert," became popular in Europe and America. But the image was overly romanticized. As noted above, Muhammad was a merchant and a townsman; so were most of his early followers. After leaving Mecca, he went to Yathrib where he preached to the peasants of that agricultural oasis. The desert nomads were late in accepting the faith of Islam. In the early centuries of the faith, they

7

were sometimes fickle believers who fomented rebellions and returned to their pre-Islamic beliefs.

Arabic speakers themselves have contributed to the image of their ancestors as free-wheeling figures urging their pure-bred stallions across the burning sands. Since the time of the Ghassanids and Lakhmids, they have carefully fostered the idea that the Bedouin was a free man who needed only his camel for travel, his horse for war, a sword, a bow, and someone to rob. But this was often a kind of nostalgia for the "good old days" in the desert. Patrons encouraged their hired poets to write in what they thought of as the Bedouin style. This led to the collection and preservation of what was supposedly the work of nomadic poets. Much as North Americans glorify the Wild West and idolize the cowpoke, the desert and the Bedouin became the objects of a romantic cult. Just as this obsession with what was really a brief and prosaic period has distorted the American image of history, so the obsession with the hard-scrabble life of peninsular nomads has distorted the image of the Prophet Muhammad, his early followers, and Islam itself.

The Faith of Islam

Islam is an Arabic word derived from a verb *salama* which has the basic meaning of "submission in order to gain peace." The word *Muslim* (variant English spelling: Moslem) describes any individual who accepts and professes Islam. The submission that a Muslim makes is to *Allah*. Allah is simply the Arabic word for "God," a cognate to the Hebrew word *Elohim*. It is not the name of a particular god like Krishna or Zeus. By submitting to God and his plan for humanity, a Muslim gains peace and contentment in this world as well as the next. According to Muslim belief, Islam is the natural religion of humanity. It is as old as humankind, since Adam, the first human, was also the first prophet of God.

8

Prophets as messengers The literal meaning of the word "prophet" is "an individual who speaks for God." Since the time of Adam, God has sent many prophets. The names of some of the prophets are familiar to those who follow the *Torah* (the Hebrew bible) and the Gospels. For instance, Abraham, or Ibrahim, is considered a major prophet as well as the founder of the Arab race. Moses (in Arabic, *Musa*), his brother Aaron (Arabic, *Harun*), Job (Arabic, *Ayub*), Elias (Arabic, *Ilyas*), and Jesus (Arabic, *Isa*) are all recognized by Muslims as prophets. In addition to the prophets familiar in the Jewish and Christian traditions, there are others known only through the revelation presented through the Prophet Muhammad: for example, the ancient Arab prophet Hud. Therefore, Muslims do not consider Muhammad to be the founder of Islam. Muhammad was the last and greatest in a long line of messengers sent by God to teach "the way of submission to God to gain peace": Islam. To refer to believers as "Muhammadans" or to their faith as "Muhammadanism" is both incorrect and insulting.

The last and greatest of the prophets Muhammad was born about A.D. 570 in the city of Mecca in the Arabian Peninsula. His father had died shortly before his birth and his mother died when he was six. He was raised by his grandfather, who died when Muhammad was nine. Then a paternal uncle, Abu Talib, looked after the boy until he reached his teens. Muhammad found employment with the merchants of Mecca and made several journeys with the caravans into Syria. Though poor, Muhammad's family had once been prominent in the city.

At age twenty-five Muhammad married Khadijah. Khadijah, wealthy in her own right, was the widow of a rich merchant. She was also some fifteen years senior to Muhammad. While she lived, Muhammad was able to find occasional periods when he could go out into the wilderness near Mecca for fasting, prayer, and meditation. About the year A.D. 610, Muhammad began receiving revelations from God transmitted through the angel Gabriel (Arabic, *Jibrail*). At first, Muhammad worried that he might be going mad, but Khadijah encouraged him by telling him that the revelations might be from God.

Once he accepted the idea that these messages came from God, Muhammad began preaching. In a sense, Muhammad was reintroducing the Arabs to Islam. Islam, its followers believe, was once the natural faith of the Arabs as of other people. However, they had entered an Age of Ignorance (*al-Jahiliyyah*) in which they no longer recognized Islam. Muhammad's mission, as this was stated in the revelations he received, was to bring Arabs back to the true faith. At first, the Meccans did not accept Muhammad's teaching. Muhammad's standing in the city made it difficult for them to do anything more than laugh or shout insults when Muhammad preached. However, they could get at his followers, especially those who were poor and those who were slaves.

Even before he began receiving revelations, Muhammad had acquired a reputation for scrupulous honesty. He was known throughout the northern portion of the peninsula by the nickname *al-Amin*, "the trustworthy." The high regard that Muhammad enjoyed outside of Mecca brought him a delegation from Yathrib. The leaders of Yathrib saw in Muhammad a possible solution for the internal conflicts that wracked their agricultural oasis. They invited the Prophet to come to Yathrib to act as a mediator between the warring factions. Muhammad's acceptance was, however, contingent on the agreement by the people of Yathrib to listen to the Prophet's message.

Muhammad left Mecca for Yathrib in A.D. 622. That event is known as the *Hijrah*, "the migration." Older

10

texts often referred to the *Hegira* as Muhammad's "flight" from Mecca. It was, as we have seen, planned in advance, with an eye toward the new opportunities it opened to the Prophet. It was not, therefore, a flight. The year of the Hijrah became the year "1" of the Muslim lunar calendar. All subsequent events were dated "A.H.," *anno Hijri,* "year of the Hijrah." Thus, the year 1985 was 1406 A.H.

After Muhammad's migration to Yathrib, the name of the town gradually changed. It became Madinah (variant spelling: Medina), meaning "the city" which was short for the phrase *Madinah al-Nabi,* "City of the Prophet." From this base, Muhammad began a series of raids and campaigns against his old enemies in Mecca. Since Mecca was dependent on trade, Muhammad had only to threaten the Meccan caravans to disrupt the life of the city. In A.D. 627, the Meccans admitted defeat. At the same time, they acknowledged their error in rejecting the Prophet and most of them accepted Islam. Muhammad entered the city in triumph. His first act was to purify the Kaabah. He removed all the idols that the desert tribes and the Meccans worshiped. The only object from the jahiliyyah which remained was a black stone (perhaps a meteorite) embedded in the foundation of the Kaabah.

Following his victory, Muhammad continued to live in Madinah. He returned to Mecca once a year to make a pilgrimage. Muhammad died of natural causes after making one of these pilgrimages in the year A.D. 632. He was buried in the courtyard of his house in Madinah.

Throughout his life, Muhammad lived in a very simple style. Stories told of him doing such mundane chores as milking his own goat and patching a tear in his cloak. He was always accessible to his followers, who could approach him with their problems or visit with him.

Later generations of Muslims looked upon the years of Muhammad's leadership in Madinah as a golden age. They believed that in his lifetime the Muslims formed a perfect community, in Arabic, *ummah*. Because everyone truly believed and acted according to the Prophet's teaching, the Muslims lived in an idyllic state. Almost all Muslims would agree that the establishment of such an ummah throughout the entire world is one of the hallmarks of God's plan for humanity.

Revelations From the beginning of his active career as a prophet, A.D. 610, until shortly before his death, Muhammad received revelations from God. According to Muslim teaching, these revelations represented a rendering of God's own book located in Heaven. These revelations were sometimes short and sometimes long. They sometimes contained general statements about the nature of the universe, God, and the purpose of human life. At other times, they referred to specific events that had taken place recently. Almost every aspect of human life was at least mentioned in these revelatory statements.

All the verses of the revelations were delivered in a kind of rhythmic prose, which cannot really be captured in English. Within ten years of the Prophet's death, a collection of all the revelations was put together in a single book known as the *Quran* (variant spelling, Koran). *Quran* meant literally "the Recitation" or "the Reading." Pious Muslims have always added some adjective to indicate the sanctity of the Book, so Muslims referred to it as *The Holy Quran* or *The Noble Quran*. The recitation of the holy book has always had a special place in the religious life of Muslims, even for those who were not speakers of Arabic. The power of its oral presentation was hinted at by Muslims who referred to recitation of the *Quran* as "lawful magic." Memorization of the text was a particularly meritorious act and those who managed it acquired the special title of *Hafiz*.

In addition to the text of the *Holy Quran*, the example of the Prophet became an important source for the Muslims' understanding of how they should practice their faith. Known as the *sunnah*, which meant the "prescribed action," it provided a model for doing such things as praying or making the pilgrimage to Mecca, but also for such things as how men should behave in the presence of women or how one should deal with one's relatives. For example, the Prophet Muhammad had a beard. Therefore, his *sunnah* encouraged Muslim males to grow beards. Indeed, having a beard was in itself a pious act.

In the first decades of the community's life, determining the sunnah was a fairly simple process. At the time of the Prophet's death, when there were about 25,000 believers, one could simply ask someone who had witnessed the Prophet's behavior. As the generation that had direct knowledge of Muhammad began to die off, leaders of the community became concerned about preserving the Prophet's sunnah. Anecdotes, stories about what the Prophet said and did, started to circulate. Each story, called in Arabic a *hadith* (plural: *ahadith*), contained two elements. The first was an *isnad*, which was a list of those individuals who had passed along the story. The second portion was the actual narration of the Prophet's saying or action. The following was fairly typical in both elements.

> Abu Yusuf said: Muhammad ibn Abi
> Ayyash told me on the authority of Anas,
> who said:
>
> The prophet of God, may God bless and
> save him, said: "Who invokes one
> blessing for me, God will repay him with

ten blessings and unburden him of ten evils."

By the late ninth century A.D., the study of hadith literature had become a specialized academic study. This was necessary in part because people started forging stories that suited their own ideas about how Muslims should behave. In the attempt by Muslim scholars to identify "sound" hadith, the isnads proved to be the most important test. For example, if one person in the chain of transmitters had died before the next in line was born, it was safe to assume that the anecdote was forged. Using this kind of simple methodology, authoritative collectors of hadith eliminated hundreds of thousands of concocted stories. After A.D. 900, six collections of hadith commanded the greatest respect among Sunni Muslims.

Collecting sound hadith did not, however, clarify all the problems that faced Muslims. In part, this resulted from the hadith's inability to address every new question that arose. As the community of believers grew, as it spread through West Asia and as non-Arabs entered the faith, issues came to the fore that were not mentioned in the holy book or the hadith. In part, the difficulty stemmed from the tendency for different hadith to put forward contradictory views. On the crucial subject of wealth, for example, the hadith spoke with several voices. One hadith praised honest toil by putting words like, "No one has ever eaten better food than that which he eats as a result of the labor of his hands," (*Sayings of Muhammad*, 20–21) in the mouth of the Prophet. Another saying, also attributed to Muhammad, took a rather different view of riches by noting that, "To leave your heirs rich is better than to leave them poor." (*Sahih Muslim*, III, 864).

In time, the community developed other methods of deciding what was appropriate behavior for a Muslim. One of these was based on the idea that when the community as a whole agreed on a particular action or belief, it was probably right. Called *ijma* in Arabic, this "consensus" of the faithful would establish the correct standard in the absence of a direct command in scripture or a clear example of the sunnah of the Prophet found in hadith. In addition to the consensus of the community, several other procedures made use of some form of independent judgment: *ijtihad* or *ray*, translated respectively as "informed opinion derived from an examination of sources" and "reason." Those attempting to establish a standard of behavior could also make use of *qiyas*, "analogy," which involved applying a solution to a problem similar to the issue one confronted. Thus, a Muslim seeking to determine which course of action would be in conformity with Islam had a method for establishing what was right. First, one consulted the *Holy Quran*. If it contained no direct command relevant to the case, one sought guidance in the sunnah of the Prophet as that was found in collections of hadith. If the sunnah did not provide a clear example, then one relied upon the consensus of the community of believers or on the informed views of an individual learned in the scripture and traditions of the Prophet and the faithful.

As with other world religions, Islam became more and more organized over time. The beliefs and actions considered essential for the practice of the faith were specified with greater clarity. That did not mean, however, that all Muslims adhered strictly to the ideal laid out in the *Quran* and sunnah. Muslims exhibited a range of behavior similar to that found among the faithful of any other religion; some were saints, others sinners, hypocrites, or lukewarm. Muslims were no more and no less attached to their faith than Christians or Jews.

Muslim Beliefs and Duties

By the eighth century, the fundamental beliefs of Muslims were basically established. The five articles of faith (*iman*) on which most of the faithful concurred were as follows:

Tawhid The oneness of God. The first portion of the Muslim creed read "There is no God, but God . . . (*la illaha illah allah*). The God referred to here was the same as that worshiped by Jews and Christians. Christians, however, spoke of God as a trinity: one God with three distinct persons. Muslims viewed that as a violation of this most fundamental belief: God is one.

God's angels Just like Jews and Christians, Muslims asserted that God created pure spiritual beings to serve as messengers (the literal meaning of "angel"). The angels were God's agents who carried the Word of God to the prophets.

The prophets of God As noted above, a number of prophets have appeared throughout human history. Muhammad was the last and was known as the "Seal of the Prophets." The second portion of the Muslim creed read, "and Muhammad is the messenger of God."

Muslims called Muhammad the Seal of the Prophets for two reasons. The first was that he confirmed everything the prophets who came before him revealed. The divine truths that they taught were the same as those taught by Muhammad. However, the followers of those prophets (not the prophets themselves) sometimes forgot the truth or corrupted it to suit their own desires. Muhammad's mission was necessary in order to correct the errors and restore what was forgotten. He was the "Seal of the Prophets" in the second sense, because he was the last prophet.

Part of Muhammad's uniqueness as a prophet was that he set the foundations for a single "community of faith (ummah)." The other prophets preached noble ideals, but the Prophet Muhammad, according to Muslim teaching, established the institutions that made it possible to live in accordance with those noble truths. His teachings on prayer, fasting, and good works were, in Muslim eyes, superior to the good intentions of Christians or Jews.

The Book God entrusted many of the prophets with a copy of the one divine book, which was with God in heaven. However, the books of the previous prophets were either lost or corrupted by later generations. This was the case with the Torah of Moses and the Gospels of Jesus. *The Holy Quran*, therefore, became the only correct copy of the heavenly book. According to Muslim belief, however, Christians and Jews, though in error, were still "people of the book." Because of that, they were entitled to special protection by the Muslims. Unlike polytheists, Jews and Christians could not be compelled to reject their errors and accept Islam. They were supposed to have the freedom to worship as they pleased and continue practices, such as drinking wine, that were contrary to Muslim custom.

The Day of Judgment Muslims, like Christians, looked forward to a "last day," when this world would be destroyed. God will sit in judgment on the souls of all those who have ever lived. Those who have been faithful and obedient to the will of God will enter paradise. Those who have rejected God and sinned will be condemned to hellfire.

While these five propositions constituted the fundamental beliefs, they did not wholly define the faith. In addition to the articles of faith, certain duties (known collectively as *din:* "religion") were incumbent upon Muslims. They were as follows:

Ibadat This word is difficult to translate into English. It referred to the "worshipful attitude" or "piety" that should characterize a believer. A Muslim should do everything in a spirit of dedication to God. Pious Muslims commonly began every task—eating meals, writing a letter, even copulation— with the phrase, "In the name of God, the beneficent, the merciful."

Salat These constituted the formal prayers that Muslims were supposed to perform. Muslims should pray five times a day. These prayers may be said privately and in any place freed from ritually-polluting substances such as blood or feces. Many pious Muslims, however, prayed with other believers, often in a mosque, the English corruption for the Arabic word for a place of public worship, *masjid*. People who missed a prayer at its appointed time could make it up later. On Friday, Muslims were encouraged to attend the noon prayer at a mosque. No sin was incurred by saying that prayer in private. Many Muslims, even those who did not pray regularly, liked to go to these Friday congregational (*jama*) prayers. In addition to the normal round of prayers, a religious scholar or a man noted for his personal piety would deliver a short sermon (*khutbah*) exhorting the believers to be faithful to God's commands.

Zakat This term referred to the "poor tax," which all Muslims should pay. The revelations of the *Quran* and the sunnah of the Prophet emphasized that alms were the *right* of the poor. *Zakat* did not mean "charity" in the Euro-American sense: money given to someone who does not deserve it because she or he was probably responsible for her or his own impoverishment. Muslims hold that the poor have a legitimate claim on the support offered by those members of the community who possess wealth. In the ideal Muslim community (ummah) the zakat would be treated as a yearly tax levied on all believers.

Though different interpretations existed, the figure of one-fortieth of an individual's net worth, not income, represented the amount that should be given to the poor, sick, or crippled.

Sawm/Rozah (The Fast) During the month of Ramadan, the name of the month during which the Prophet received his first revelations, Muslims who were not incapacitated by illness, advanced age, youth, or the necessities of travel, fasted completely, taking no food, water, and tobacco in the hours between sunrise and sunset. Muslims were supposed to avoid any pleasurable activity during that time. In some areas of the Muslim world, the government and popular pressure enforced the fast strictly. In others, it was not so scrupulously observed. Muslims who kept the fast, however, enjoyed the respect even of those who failed to do so. Among uneducated poor Muslims who needed to engage in physical labor, which makes fasting impossible, those who observed the fast were considered "lucky."

Despite the hardships imposed by the fast, Ramadan evenings were times of celebration. Families visited relatives and friends, held festive dinners, and enjoyed special religious gatherings such as recitations of the *Quran* or religious poetry. For Muslims, two major feasts (*ids*) were traditional. The first id marked the end of the month of fasting. During the holiday, people distributed special foods, especially sweets, and gave gifts of clothing.

Hajj *Hajj* referred to the pilgrimage to Mecca. All Muslims who can afford it should make the pilgrimage to Mecca once in their lives. Those who have fulfilled this duty received particular recognition in their communities and added the title *Hajji* to their names. Because it gave Muslims the opportunity to come into close contact with believers from all over the world, the pilgrimage was always a most significant reminder of the international character of Islam.

Jihad At present, European and American news media have paid a lot of attention to this aspect of Islamic faith. Journalists have translated *Jihad* as "Holy War." That translation is completely misleading. Jihad derives from a word meaning "struggle." In the daily life of the average pious Muslim, Jihad was the constant struggle to "avoid evil and do good." Thus, it resembles the Christian injunction to "fight temptation." This personal quest was called the "Greater Jihad."

What the newspapers have commonly called Holy War is the "Lesser Jihad." This usage emphasizes the duty of all believers to give their lives in defense of the true faith. When evil threatens the truth, all believers should be prepared to forfeit their lives to preserve the Word of God. It is no different from the Christian message that the faithful should lay down their lives in order that they may live in Christ. To Muslims, the emphasis in Jihad is defensive rather than offensive. The word Jihad would be better translated as Holy Martyrdom rather than Holy War.

Later Religious Developments

Laid out in bold-faced headings the faith of Islam seems remarkably simple. However, in matters of daily living the attempt to "do the good and avoid the evil" is no easier for Muslims than for any other people in the world. Conflicts have emerged between different interpretations of the faith. Also, different styles of piety have developed.

Learned scholars of religion As a class of religious scholars began to form, a rigorous textbook version of Islam became associated with these learned men (*ulama*). The word "ulama," often mistranslated as "Islamic clergy," derived from the Arabic word for "knowledge": *ilm*. This was a particular kind of knowledge, knowledge of the religious sciences such as the study of hadith, the interpretation of the *Holy*

Quran (*tafsir*), theology (*kalam*),and the systematic application of the tests of Muslim behavior described above (*fiqh*). By the year A.D. 1000, scholars were becoming more and more specialized in the study of one or another branch of these religious sciences. Thus, the ulama were, literally, "those who have knowledge."

The ulama took as their special preserve the subject called *shariah*. This word has often been translated as Islamic Law, but once again the common translation was not always the most correct. The shariah, which meant "the path, the way," involved all the things that a pious Muslim should do. Since many of those were by nature unenforceable as law, the word really should be translated as the "Islamic guide to the conscience" or "Islamic ways of life." Some aspects of the shariah were too detailed for ordinary believers, but the religious scholars always did their best to follow every prescription and to criticize anyone who did not. Often these individuals, the shariah-minded or piety-minded, were a lonely minority who found themselves in conflict not only with the way the masses actually lived, but with the kings and warriors who ruled Muslim states. Kings often found the prescriptions of the scholars too inconvenient for the smooth operation of government.

The Sufis Another style of religious behavior that became very popular in the Muslim world was associated with individuals called *Sufis*. *Sufi* derived from a word meaning "wool cloak." The first Sufis were often highly critical of the luxury in which the rich lived. To show their disdain, they wore a humble wool coat, usually patched with different colored bits of cloth. The Sufis often encouraged a personal, emotional commitment to the love of God. They sometimes made fun of the religious scholars, accusing them of hypocrisy. As one Sufi-inspired poem put it,

> Were there wine and privacy and the fair
>   face of one's beloved
> Swear an oath, oh Puritan!, if you were
>   there, what would you do?

(Barker 1: 113)

Mansur al-Hallaj, an early tenth-century Sufi, was a classic example of the wandering holy man whose own religious passions set him apart from the ulama and shocked conventional believers. Al-Hallaj expressed the impact of his personal experience in the following:

> Hide me from God, you people! Hide me
> from God! He took me from myself and
> has not given me back; and I cannot
> perform the service I should in His
> presence for my fear of His leaving me
> alone again. He will leave me deserted,
> abandoned! and woe for the man who
> knows himself outcast after that Presence!

(Kritzeck 95)

Implicit in al-Hallaj's statement was the assertion that he had in fact seen God. On another occasion, he uttered a phrase that became famous in the Muslim world, *Ana'l-Haqq:* "I am the truth," in effect saying, "I am God." Al-Hallaj was indicating that his personal experience of God had merged his personality with the being of the One. Al-Hallaj knew what the consequences of such views would be.

> I have renounced the Faith of God.
> Obligatory on me:
> It was to do what for Belief
> would be iniquity.
>
> God had made me an outlaw. Kill me.

No task is more urgent for Muslims at
this moment than my execution.
Realize this, that my death will preserve
the sanctions of the Law; he who has
offended must undergo them.

(Kritzeck 97)

In A.D. 922 , al-Hallaj met the death he begged for.
Oddly enough, he was not punished for having
completely identified himself with God, but for saying
that Muslims need not make the pilgrimage to Mecca,
that they could walk around their own homes and get
the same benefit. For that he was beaten, had a hand
and a foot amputated, was crucified, beheaded, and his
body burned. The Sufi movement, however,
continued to grow. Within a few centuries, statements
similar to al-Hallaj's became commonplace and
accepted as a valid poetic metaphor. Sufis became
organized in hundreds of "orders" (*tariqat*)
distinguished from one another primarily by different
"chains" (*silsilah*) linking generations of Sufi teachers
and their disciples.

Famous Sufis often acquired a reputation as
"friends of God" who were able to intercede with the
creator to provide ordinary people with one or another
blessing. For example, barren women who wanted
children would approach one of these "friends" in the
hope that they would be able to become fertile. A poor
farmer whose ox had died might come to the holy man
hoping that he could arrange a miracle whereby the
money for a new ox would appear. In time, many Sufi
"saints" became known for their ability to work these
wonders. Even after a saint's death, the power did not
disappear. The tombs of such saints became popular
pilgrimage centers. All over West, South, and
Southeast Asia, the veneration of Sufi saints became

the most common way in which ordinary Muslims expressed their faith.

Toward a Muslim Philosophy

As the Arabs established an empire in West Asia they came into contact with the traditions of Hellenistic civilization. The impact of Hellenism was most visible in Islamic architecture. The arches and domes, which characterize many mosques and other buildings, were adapted from the Hellenistic style. Less obvious than architectural forms, but equally significant, were intellectual disciplines, which had been nurtured in the Hellenistic cities and which Muslims eventually preserved.

The Hellenistic tradition At first, Muslims were most interested in the practical sciences of medicine and astrology/astronomy. In the Hellenistic tradition, however, there was no absolute separation between science and philosophy.

The same individuals usually pursued more than one subject and intermixed metaphysical speculation with discourses on disease or the implications of planetary motion. Muslims soon began to dabble in philosophy. Al-Kindi, an Arab who died about A.D. 873 was the first Muslim recognized as a "philosopher." The Arabic term used for his field of study was *falsafah,* obviously a version of the Greek word *philosophia.* Those who specialized in the teachings of the "ancients" that is, the Greek thinkers like Plato and Aristotle, bore a name that was also borrowed from the Greek language: *failasuf.* Al-Kindi was followed by a number of Muslim philosophers whose ethnic background reflected the spread of the Islamic faith to non-Arabs. Al-Farabi, whose ancestors were Turks, was the first Muslim philosopher to expand upon the basic doctrines of the ancient Greeks.

After al-Farabi's death in 950, a number of other thinkers, who became well known in Europe during the "Middle Ages," took up a study of philosophy. Though many Muslims contributed to the explication of the classical Greek thinkers, only a few have remained famous to present-day Euro-Americans. Ibn-Sina, an Iranian who died in 1037, achieved a certain amount of notoriety in Europe under the Latinized version of his name, Avicenna. Ibn-Sina was a physician, a chemist, and a philosopher. He wrote an encyclopedia, which attempted to record all there was to know on every topic of human knowledge. A Spanish philosopher, Ibn-Rushd, called by medieval Europeans Averroes, was by the end of his life in 1198 recognized as one of the most perceptive interpreters of the Greek philosopher Aristotle.

These thinkers did more than preserve and repeat the ideas they learned from the Hellenistic philosophers. They provided new insights into the views of the masters as well as adapting classical philosophy to the requirements of the age in which they lived. In this work, Muslims were joined by both Christian and Jewish thinkers. Often, Christians acted as the translators for Arabic-speaking Muslims. Some of them were able to translate from Syriac into Arabic, while a few actually knew classical Greek and went directly from that language to Arabic without a Syriac intermediary. Some of the greatest Jewish philosophers, notably Moses Maimonides (d. 1204), lived and worked among Muslims. Sometimes they wrote in Arabic or composed their books in the Hebrew language written in Arabic letters.

The cooperation of Christians, Jews, and Muslims illustrated the cosmopolitan character of Islamic civilization. The character of the civilization was not wholly the product of the faith of Islam. Many non-Muslims contributed to it and employed its civilizational forms. Up until the present day, large communities of Christians, Jews, and Zoroastrians have survived in the Muslim world, usually, with some notable exceptions, living peacefully among the Muslim majority.

The theologians In part, because it was associated with the pagan Greeks as well as with Jews and Christians, philosophy in its pure form aroused the suspicions of theologians. After all, philosophy called upon people to use reason to investigate the ultimate realities of the universe. Like Christianity, Islam relied on simple faith: "I believe, though I do not understand how."

Al-Ashari, who died in 936, studied philosophical theology as a young man, but when he reached maturity, he began to attack the philosophers. His aim seems to have been to find a middle way between the rationalism of the philosophers and the blind faith of the theologians. That both groups thought of him as a traitor indicated that he probably succeeded.

Al-Ghazali, who died in 1111, was a more influential critic of the philosophers. Like al-Ashari, he studied philosophy in his youth, but later turned his back on this mode of thinking in favor of a position closer to that of the theologians. He summed up his harsh views in a work called the *Tahafut al-Falasifah* (The Incoherence of the Philosophers). Although Ibn-Rushd attempted to answer al-Ghazali with a work known as the *Tahafut al-Tahafut* (The Incoherence of the Incoherence), al-Ghazali's views tended to dominate among Muslim religious thinkers.

Studies of the libraries, writings, and lectures of religious scholars indicate that many of those who were accepted as models of theological orthodoxy continued to study the ancient Greeks and their Muslim commentators in private. As a religion, Islam has never been quite as rigid as Europeans and Americans thought. Indeed, one important element of Greek philosophy survived in even the most narrow theological circles. The study of dialectical logic (*mantiq*) remained an important part of the course of study for any aspiring theologian.

Al-Ghazali was a major figure in more ways than one. He became interested in the Sufi path to direct communion with God. He found Sufi masters willing to teach him and he worked out, in his own person rather than in a systematic theological form, a union between the ecstatic, emotional approach of the Sufis and the drier, firmer path followed by the theologians.

Europeans and Americans have always assumed that the Muslims were somehow more committed to their faith than Christians and Jews. Dwelling on the intricacies of the debate between philosophers and theologians has probably reinforced that impression. However, one must remember that religious faith seldom eliminates common sense. Reality is as complicated for Muslims as it is for anyone else. An old Persian proverb reflects this practical emphasis. It goes, "Trust in God, but tie up your camel."

In discussing the intricacies of the faith of Islam and the civilization that developed in West Asia and elsewhere in the world, the political history of the area in the years following the death of the Prophet Muhammad has not yet been mentioned. While matters of faith and philosophy seem important, the intellectual and cultural movements outlined above took place in the context of a major political change in West Asia.

II
The Emergence of the Arab Empire

At the time of Muhammad's death in A.D. 632, about 25,000 people professed their faith in Islam. While the Prophet lived, their ideal had been to live in a true ummah, a community of faith in which all members were equal, living according to the revelations contained in the *Holy Quran* and in imitation of the practice of the Prophet. Almost by accident, however, these people soon found themselves at the head of a vast empire, which included the territories that had once been part of the Sassanid state and others that had been ruled by the Eastern Roman Empire of the Byzantines. Nothing in the scriptures or in the living example of Muhammad's life prepared them for these events. The worldly power and wealth that some members of the community came to control began to create tensions between the high ideals of the faith and the inequalities that accompanied the uneven distribution of material goods as well as political influence.

Rule by the Caliphs

After the Prophet died, his closest followers decided to name a "successor" (*khalifah*, English variant: "caliph"). The caliph was not in any sense a successor to Muhammad as a prophet; rather he was supposed to direct the temporal affairs of the faithful. For example, while he lived the Prophet had commanded the troops in battle, settled disputes among the faithful, and given advice on everything from domestic relations to sound business practices. The caliph was supposed to take over these functions. Thus, he was not analogous to the pope in Roman Catholicism, nor was he exactly like a king. Indeed, the first caliphs ruled because of the prestige they enjoyed as close friends of Muhammad and their reputations for personal piety.

An old man and his army Abu Bakr, the first caliph, was an old man. He faced several problems. The faithful were accustomed to following the orders of the Prophet himself. Some of the believers, especially among the desert tribesmen, considered Islam a matter of personal agreement between themselves and Muhammad. With his death, they considered themselves relieved of their obligations and rebelled. Partly in order to keep these rebels quiet, Abu Bakr ordered several raiding parties to attack Syria and Palestine and Iraq. What no one envisioned was that the small armies dispatched would be successful. In September of A.D. 635, for example, the ancient city of Damascus surrendered to an Arab army. This city would eventually become the capital of the caliphate. In quick succession, Palestine, including the city of Jerusalem, Egypt, and parts of Iran fell into Arab hands. Following the battle of al-Qadasiyah in A.D. 637, the Sassanid Empire disintegrated rapidly. The Arabs found themselves ruling over vast territories and non-Arab populations that outnumbered them.

The success of the Arab armies was due in part to the internal weakness of both the Sassanid and Byzantine states. They had been fighting each other for almost two hundred years; their treasuries, their armies, and their ability to mobilize the willing cooperation of their subjects were exhausted. Also, sizeable numbers of people living in those two empires had reason to desire the fall of the government. In the Byzantine Empire, Christian sects like the Nestorians and Monophysites had experienced religious persecution at the hands of imperial soldiers. In Iran, the peasants had long before wearied of oppressive taxation. They were equally disturbed by the occasional persecutions of religious or ethnic minorities.

For most of these people, the Arabs appeared as liberators. For their part, the early Arab rulers often reduced the tax burdens of the peasants. Finally, the Arab armies were aided by the Arabs who were settled as farmers or merchants in the areas they conquered. Though many of these Arabs were Christians rather than Muslims, they seemed willing to help their ethnic cousins rather than the Byzantines or Persians. Within thirty years of Muhammad's death, this empire included territory that ran from Egypt to the edge of the Central Asian steppe and from the Arabian Peninsula to the border of Anatolia.

Empire management While the generals and the soldiers in the Arab armies that managed those dramatic victories were usually desert nomads, the leadership of the Muslim community remained in the hands of men who were urban merchants by background. Their experience as townsmen and traders gave them little guidance in the management of empires based on peasant agriculture. Also, the Arab cultural tradition provided them with few precedents of how kings should function.

At Abu Bakr's death, the closest followers of the Prophet once again selected an old companion of the Prophet, Umar, as caliph. At Umar's death, they chose a man named Uthman as successor. Uthman had not been among the early members of the community. He belonged to a Meccan family that was among the last to accept Muhammad's prophethood. This family, however, did have close connections with Damascus, the city that was fast becoming more important than Muhammad's old headquarter's town, Madinah. Uthman reigned as caliph for twelve years (A.D. 644-656). During the second half of Uthman's caliphate some of the problems created by the rapid expansion of the Arab Empire became manifest.

Uthman, like any good merchant, had relied on his family to rule the empire. His cousins and other relatives received the command of armies and the governorships of the various provinces. This caused some discontent among those who had been early supporters of the Prophet. Another source of discontent stemmed from the method of rewarding the soldiers in the army. In the first years of the conquest, goods taken as booty were shared out equally among all the troops. But new soldiers who joined up got the same amount as the veterans who had been serving for a longer period. In 656, a group of disgruntled soldiers marched on Madinah to present their grievances, rioted there, dragged Uthman out of his home, and killed him.

Divisions

The death of Uthman became the occasion for a serious division among Muslims, which remains significant to the present. After the caliph's murder, the people of Madinah selected a man named Ali as successor. Ali, a first cousin of the Prophet, married the only living child of Muhammad, Fatimah. Thus, Ali and Fatimah's sons, Hasan and Husain, were the Prophet's grandsons. In addition to his ties of kinship to the Prophet, Ali enjoyed a reputation for exceptional piety and a profound understanding of Islam.

Not everyone accepted Ali as caliph. Muawiyyah, the governor of Syria, commander of that province's army and cousin of Uthman, opposed Ali's selection. He gathered his army and began the march from Damascus toward Ali's capital at Kufa. Ali, for his part, collected an army to defend his rights. Before the armies could fight a decisive battle, soldiers of the Syrian army suggested that some kind of compromise be worked out. Those chosen as representatives by Ali and Muawiyyah appeared to be interested in delaying a decision as long as possible. During the interval of waiting, Ali was assassinated by a former soldier in his army who was convinced that Ali had "sold out" by agreeing to arbitration. With Ali's death in January of 661, Muawiyyah became the caliph by default.

Shiites and Sunnis Muawiyyah's succession led to two important changes in the character of the Arab empire and the faith of Islam. The first caused a split between those who were partisans of Ali, known in Arabic as *Shiah al-Ali* (Shiite is the common Anglicized version of this Arabic phrase meaning "party of Ali") and those who were willing to accept any pious Muslim as the leader of the community. Some years after Ali's death, both his sons, Hasan and Husain, attempted to claim the caliphate by right of their descent from the Prophet Muhammad. The first of them died under house arrest in Madinah, while Husain died a martyr's death at a place called Karbala.

After the death of Husain, the Shiite movement went underground. Though it occasionally inspired rebellion and even formed the basis for the appeal of the Fatimid rulers of Egypt (909–1171), it remained the faith of a minority of Muslims. Moreover, what began as an argument over the political leadership of the Arab Empire became over the centuries a full-fledged theological split. The beliefs of the Shiites diverged from those of other Muslims.

Shiites believe Ali compiled the *Quran* and that he was the true keeper of the words of the Prophet. Most importantly, they believe Ali was not just the fourth Caliph, but the first *Imam*.

Where Sunnis get religious guidance from *ijma*, the consensus of the community with some guidance by the *ulama*, the Shiites believe the Imam is infallible and they accept his authority unquestioningly. That fundamental difference is the major division between the two great branches of Islam.

There has not been an Imam since the twelfth Imam, Muhamad al Muntazar, who disappeared mysteriously in the late ninth century A.D. Devout Shiites believe he is still among them in a state of "occultation" and will return as the *Mahdi*, the "expected one." None since have been recognized as Imam, though from time to time religious leaders are given the title and nearly as much authority. The most recent was the Ayatollah Ruhollah Khomeini, called Imam by some of his followers and undisputed religious and secular ruler of Iran until his death in 1989.

The violent deaths of Ali and of his son Husain, the second Imam, have left Shiites with a fixation on martyrdom and suffering as paths to paradise. These passionate traits exist to this day and stand in contrast to the legalistic formalism and dispassionate traits exhibited by the Sunni Muslims.

The Shiite movement itself split up into a number of sects and gave rise to such religions as that of the Druze, no longer considered Islamic. Those Muslims who did not belong to the Shiites were generally referred to as Sunni (short for an Arabic phrase *Ahl al-sunnah wa jamaat*, meaning "The people of the practice and community of the Prophet"). Sunni was, however, a residual category, because Sunnis exhibit a variety of religious beliefs and orientations.

Caliphs, by right of inheritance The second development, which occurred as a consequence of Muawiyyah's victory, involved the way in which caliphs were chosen. Muawiyyah introduced the dynastic principle, and thereafter, caliphs claimed their place by right of inheritance from a father, uncle, or cousin.

Muawiyyah's line of descendants were known as the Umayyads, taking the name of the family. The Umayyads ruled until A.D. 750 , when they were replaced by another caliphal dynasty, the Abbasids, who claimed to be descended from Abbas, Muhammad's uncle. The Holy Book and the practice of the Prophet did not approve or condemn the idea that the leadership of the Muslim community should pass on by right of descent. Also, in order to find models for kingly behavior, both the Umayyads and the Abbasids looked outside of the Islamic tradition to the practice of the kings of Persia. Many pious Muslims looked with suspicion on the worldly ways of both the Umayyads and Abbasids. They did not usually express their discontent by rebellion; rather they tended to go about their business leaving government to the warriors and princes.

Other potentially disruptive changes came in the years of the Umayyad and Abbasid caliphs. By that time, the living memory of Muhammad's life and example began to fade. Like other religions, notably Christianity, Islam had to find institutions that would preserve the faith and take care of passing it on to succeeding generations. While this organization of the faith was effective, belief lost some of its immediacy. Like Christianity, Islam began to experience a series of renewal movements that sought to inspire believers with the sense of commitment that characterized the early days of the community. Tensions between those who liked things as they were and those who wanted Muslims more dedicated to their religion became a common feature of Muslim history.

A second source of difficulty occurred as the Arab Muslims began living in towns. When they first conquered West Asia, the armies established camps that kept them apart from the cities of the region. As the years went by, those camps, Fustat in Egypt or Kufa in Iraq for example, became cities in themselves. The Arab population gradually settled in, some becoming peasant farmers, others shopkeepers or artisans in the cities, still others government officials. In the cities they began to imitate the behavior of other urban elites. All Muslims were supposed to be equals, but the differences of wealth that emerged made it possible for some Muslims to assert their control over others. The sense that all believers formed a single community became harder to maintain. Many pious Muslims started to condemn the luxuries of urban life, even though Islam remained an essentially urbanized religion.

Non-Arabs The third major trend concerned the place of non-Arabs in Islam. At first, the Umayyads' caliphs actually discouraged the conversion of non-Arabs, but so many of the natives of Iran, Egypt, Palestine, and Syria sought to join the faith that it proved impossible to keep them out. In the final years of the Umayyads' rule, these converts, who were usually treated as second class Muslims, began to agitate for better treatment. The support that they gave the Abbasids was crucial to that dynasty's success in ousting the Umayyads. By the year 1000, non-Arabs probably outnumbered Arabs.

While non-Arabs were joining the religion, other non-Arabs were entering the empire as immigrants and slaves. Peoples of the Central Asian steppe moved into the lands of the caliphate. Some of them continued their pastoral nomadic way of life, others came into the cities. As for the slaves, most of them were used as soldiers. When the initial conquests were over, the Bedouin who formed the nucleus of the army either became settled in the newly acquired territories or returned to the Arabian Peninsula. The caliphs felt the need to have a standing army under their personal control. To obtain this they began purchasing slaves, usually Turkish-speaking steppe nomads, who acted as soldiers. These Turkish speakers eventually came to control the Abbasid caliphs and to set up their own kingdoms at the expense of caliphal authority. Thus, the prevalence of non-Arabs, combined with the increasing importance of foreign slave-soldiers contributed to a shift in the Islamic world's center of gravity. The lands away from the Arabian Peninsula became more important. While the cities of Mecca and Madinah remained religiously significant, other places became the cultural and political capitals of the Islamic world.

III
The Islamic Middle Periods, 1000–1500 A.D.

After 1000 A.D. the Islamic world began to experience a shift in its political and cultural center of gravity. The Ummayad Caliphate was initially concentrated on the Arab world. Expansion into North Africa and Spain was accompanied by an Arabization at least of the elites of those regions. The change in capital from Madinah to Damascus did not alter that. The Abbasids who led a revolution which overthrew the Ummayads in 750 A.D. came from Khorasan, the easternmost region of Iran. Their connections to that place inspired a number of important trends.

In order to be closer to their original power base, the Abbasids built their capital at Baghdad. Baghdad, which means "Garden of Justice," was a splendid new city. Through it the Abbasids hoped to distance themselves from their Ummayad predecessors. The Abbasids eventually acquired a reputation for their wealth, the grace of their court and enlightened administration. The popular legends which formed the basis for the *One Thousand and One Arabian Nights* paid special homage to the Caliph Harun al-Rashid, turning the name of Baghdad into a synonym for a paradise on earth. But Harun al-Rashid's reputation was probably enhanced by the ineptitude and weakness of his successors. In the tenth century A.D., the Abbasid caliphs became nearly powerless, the pawns of one or another military strongman. Some of the warriors were Iranians by birth; others were Turks.

Political Decentralization

The Iranian family of the Buwayhids, also know as the Buyids, came from obscure social origins. Their father, it was said, had been a fisherman on the

Caspian Sea who became a successful soldier. The Buwayhids came to power as leaders of bands of tough Persian infantrymen hailing from the mountains of Daylam, a district southwest of the Caspian Sea. In the tenth century they held a dominant position in Baghdad, turning the caliphs into their puppets. Their religious sympathies leaned toward the Shiite sect, and they had a certain disdain for Arab political traditions.

As foot soldiers, the Daylamites were effective only when they combined forces with mounted warriors. The Abbasid caliphs had begun the tradition of recruiting cavalry from places outside their empire. Traditionally, the caliphal armies had been composed of distinct units of horsemen, often members of the same Arab tribe, brought into the army under their own commanders. The loyalty of those soldiers was often focused on their leaders and not the caliphs. In order to counteract that weakness, the Abbasids created armies composed largely of Turkish-speaking nomads from the Central Asian Steppe. These individuals were often prisoners of war captured during the many intertribal conflicts of that region. Their captors took them into Abbasid domains and sold them as slaves. Other would-be soldiers apparently sold themselves in order to gain access into the Abbasids' fabled kingdom.

Technically these nomadic soldiers were slaves. However, slavery in the Muslim world must not be confused with the style of slavery associated with the American South. Slave status was mostly a legal fiction designed to ensure the loyalty of soldiers to the commanders. No social stigma was attached to being a slave. Many of them rose to high government positions; some became rulers in their own right.

As the alliance of Daylamites and Turks controlled Baghdad, the various provinces of the Abbasid empire began to break away. The farther away from Baghdad they were, the more likely it was that governors would become independent. These nominal servants of the caliphs may have continued to respect the Abbasids in a ceremonial fashion. From time to time they may have sent the caliphs gifts or letters demanding the award of one or another honorary title, but in all practical matters they were independent.

Rebirth of Persian culture The decentralization of the Abbasid state also allowed the rebirth of Persian culture. While the Arabs had always been interested in Persian ideas about government and the rights of kings, they had no interest in other aspects of the language and culture of Persian-speaking periods. Following the Arab conquest of the Sassanian empire, little, if anything, was written in Persian. But in the tenth century A.D, partly with the encouragement of semi-autonomous rulers in Iran, "New Persian" made its appearance. New Persian was written in the Arabic script modified to represent sounds, such as "p," which did not occur in Arabic. The grammar of the language remained Indo-European, but it incorporated a great deal of Arabic vocabulary. Poetry in New Persian became a vehicle for the expression of a renewed pride in a distinctly Iranian cultural identity.

In particular, the name of the poet Abul Qasim Firdawsi became associated with the rebirth of Iranian letters. In the last years of the tenth century and the first of the eleventh, he composed the *Shahnamah*, the *Book of Kings*, which soon acquired the status of the Persian national epic. Firdawsi drew on the mythology and history of pre-Islamic Iran. As the title implies, the poem concentrated on Iranian kings and various heroes and heroines associated with them. Also, a number of its tales dealt with Alexander the Great or the famous Sassanid king Anushiravan the Just. Firdawsi rarely mentioned Islam in his poem; indeed, some of its passages slighted the faith and the Arabs who thought themselves its guardians. The *Shahnamah's* influence extended far beyond Iran. For many of the Central Asian peoples entering the

Muslim world, Persian became the language of high culture and the *Book of Kings* a source of models for royal behavior. Turkish rulers sponsored Persian poets and prose writers. Also, they usually carried on government business in Persian, relying on Persian-speaking secretaries to take care of diplomatic correspondence as well as the revenue administration of their states.

The Ghaznavids The kingdom of the Ghaznavids illustrated a number of the developments outlined above. As Abbasid control disintegrated, their nominal governors in eastern Iran—a family known as the Samanids—became independent of Baghdad. Since their territories bordered on the Central Asian Steppe, they found it easy to build an army made up largely of Turkish horsemen. Some of these "slave-soldiers" rose to responsible positions in the Samanid government. Eventually, one of them named Alptigin (a typically Turkish name) displaced the Samanids and declared himself the ruler with the title of *Sultan*, a word which literally meant, "one who has authority." Alptigin had no male heirs, but he married his daughter to a fellow slave and close associate, Sebuktigin. When Alptigin died, his son-in-law became the Sultan. In turn, Sebuktigin's son was Sultan Mahmud, who acquired legendary status—not always for his goodness—in Muslim history.

Mahmud tried to make his capital, Ghazna, located in what is now Afghanistan, one of the greatest cities of the Muslim world. He offered lavish patronage to the greatest scholars and writers of his time. If one of them refused his offer, Mahmud was not above having him kidnapped and brought by force to Ghazna. That was the way that Mahmud acquired the services of al-Biruni, one of the greatest minds of that period, who eventually wrote a work on India which is still regarded as a masterpiece.

As a patron of the arts, Mahmud enticed Firdawsi, the author of the *Shahnamah*, to his court. Legends told that Mahmud offered Firdawsi a gold coin for every couplet of the *Shahnamah*. But when Mahmud discovered that there were already 30,000 couplets and that Firdawsi was still writing, he tried to back away from his promise. Instead, he presented the poet with 30,000 silver coins. Firdawsi was so offended that he left Ghazna and died shortly afterwards of frustration. A satirical preface attributed to Firdawsi sometimes appeared at the beginning of the *Shahnamah*. The verse pillories Mahmud not only for his parsimony, but also for his sexual preference for slave boys.

Sultan Mahmud needed vast wealth to maintain his glittering court. He sometimes procured this by sending his armies across the Hindu Kush mountains to raid India. There, they would plunder a few temples and return to Ghazna laden with jewels. Apart from bankrolling Mahmud, these expeditions set a precedent for Muslim conquerors for the next six centuries and led to Islam's becoming a major force in South Asia.

The Seljuks

In addition to rulers who were originally military slaves or the descendents of slaves, free Turks, often traveling in tribal groups, came to power in Muslim West Asia. Early in the eleventh century the Seljuks, a family belonging to the Oghuz tribe, left Central Asia and moved slowly westward. By 1038 A.D., less than three decades after their migration, the Seljuks founded a series of dynasties which ruled over much of what became Iran, Iraq, Syria and Turkey until the Mongol conquests of the thirteenth century. In 1071 A.D., at Manzikert, the Seljuks administered a crushing defeat to the Byzantine army. Though the Eastern Roman empire struggled on for another 400 years, it never again had the power it did before

Manzikert. The Seljuks then began the slow process of turning Anatolia into a heartland for Turkish-speaking Muslims, a task the Ottoman emperors finally completed.

Free Turks like the Seljuks converted to Islam by slow and easy stages. While still nomadic, they retained many of the pre-Islamic beliefs and practices. Before Islam, shamans were the chief religious figures for many Central Asians. Shamans were men and women possessed by spirits or gods. They could use their spiritual power either to help or to harm people. Shamans often behaved in unusual ways, but that only seemed to add to their supernatural aura. The wandering Sufi holymen who brought Islam to the Turks also claimed superhuman powers. Their eccentric ways often resembled those of shamans. They merely asserted that these things came from the One God rather than from ghosts or nature spirits. When the Seljuks began to rule over settled populations and cities where Muslim religious scholars were well established, they had to adapt themselves to more formalized Islamic belief and practices.

Turkish rulers also inherited a certain tension between the demands of Islam as a religious faith and the concept of kingship. Since Islam asserts that God alone is the "possessor of the earth," for any human to claim power in his own right is blasphemy. The Ummayads considered themselves divinely sanctioned rulers, but the Shiites never accepted them. Likewise, the Abbasids initially seemed inclined to the Shiite cause, but they quickly abandoned it in favor of the Sunnis. In their personal lives, some Ummayad and Abbasid rulers behaved in distinctly un-Islamic ways so that many pious Sunnis condemned, in private at least, even the caliphs. Ghaznavid and Seljuk sultans were not caliphs, so any religious sanction for their rule was dubious. These sultans, therefore, often sponsored the building of mosques and theological schools (*madrasahs*), and they developed close relationships with religious scholars as well as Sufis in order to make a public display of their faith. Nevertheless, many learned and holy men refused to have anything to do with temporal rulers. They preferred to uphold the pure standards of Islam unsullied by political compromises. While many sultans were truly pious, others merely went through the motions.

Turkish culture In cultural terms, Turkish sultans quickly embraced the revived Persianate style. Persian was the language of their administration. One Seljuk minister of state, known by his title as *Nizam al-Mulk* (literally, "organizer of the kingdom") composed a work, *The Book of Government*, which became a classic of Persian literature, but also a model for many subsequent books offering advice on government and personal behavior to sultans. Nizam al-Mulk's work contained anecdotes about other kings meant to make the sultan a more effective ruler. It contained chapters on practical matters, such as how to investigate the doings of subordinate officials, as well as advice on whom the sultan should select as friends.

At first, many Arabs condemned the Turks' acquisition of power. They referred to a supposed hadith of the Holy Prophet, "If the Arabs are humbled, Islam is humbled." (Lewis, 2, 195) But, in time, this negative reaction diminished. As early as the eleventh century one scholar described the situation in the following way.

> I have seen that God caused the sun of
> empire to rise in the mansions of the
> Turks, and turned the heavenly spheres
> around their dominion, and named them
> "Turk," and gave them sovereignty, and
> made them kings of the age, and placed
> reins of the people of this time in their

hands, and ordained them over mankind,
and sustained them in the right and
strengthened those who join them and
strive for them and attain fulfillment
through them. . . . It is incumbent on
every man of sense to rally to them. . .

(Lewis, 2, 207-208)

Perso-Turkish Ascendance After 1000 A.D. an
"Eastward shift" occurred in Islam's political and
cultural heartland. This period began an age of "Perso-
Turkish Ascendance" in the Muslim world. As the
language of sacred scripture, Arabic remained
important for theology and scientific writing, but
Persian became the premier language of government,
polite society and literature. Islam's eastward
movement continued and the faith, as well as Islamic
civilization and political traditions, spread to India,
China and the Indonesian-Philippine archipelago.
Arabic speakers became a minority within the Muslim
world. Of the currently one billion Muslims, only
about 150 million are Arabs. They are far outnumbered
by speakers of Javanese, Bengali, Urdu, Persian and
Turkish.

The Pax Mongolica

In the popular imagination, the Mongols represent
the classic barbarian invaders. While the initial
Mongol forays of the thirteenth century, together with
the subsequent invasions of Timur in the fourteenth,
did bring death and destruction, the Mongols did not
fit completely the legendary stereotypes. For one thing,
many of those involved in the invasions were not
Mongols, but speakers of Turkish languages. They had
many connections to earlier waves of Turkish
immigrants and rulers. They were, therefore, already
more than half-civilized when they arrived in the
Muslim West.

Temugin, better known as *Chinggiz Khan* (literally, 'the world lord") began life in difficult circumstances. His father, the chief of a small tribe which spoke a Mongolian language, had been killed while Temugin was a child. He was forced to wander the steppes almost alone. Temugin, however, eventually came to believe that God, called by the Mongols "The Great Sky," had selected him to pacify the world. After regaining leadership of his tribe, Temugin began to build a coalition of other Mongolian and Turkish-speaking tribes. In religious terms, they were a diverse group. Some had been Christianized; others were Muslims; still others were Buddhists, while many—like Temugin—retained their faith in the spirits of the sky, earth and mountains. Whatever their faith, they all seem to have accepted the idea that Temugin had a divine calling. They followed him, both to the east into China and to the west into the Muslim heartland. Thus Temugin became Chinggiz Khan.

As they embarked on their conquests, the Mongols demanded the instant submission of any peoples or cities they encountered. If they surrendered, the Mongols incorporated them into their confederacy. In that way, Chinggiz soon acquired the services of many Persian and Chinese administrators. However, if they met with any resistance, the Mongols applied swift and pitiless violence. Previous conquerors had contented themselves with taking cities and leaving the peasants of the surrounding regions alone. Being horse-soldiers, the Mongols had no patience for long sieges. When dealing with a recalcitrant city, the Mongol army would fan out into the countryside and force all the people they found there to do the work of besieging the city for them. The defenders of the city thus found themselves killing the peasants who had provided their food supply. When a city finally fell, the Mongols made an example of it by killing most of the inhabitants. They sometimes forced a few craftsmen

45

and artists to relocate to Mongol domains, but the rest were slaughtered. Cities which existed before the Mongol incursions ceased being inhabited. Perhaps more importantly, vast stretches of agricultural land were left empty.

In 1258 A.D., Hulugu Khan, the grandson of Chinggiz, approached the city of Baghdad. The citizens pretended they would surrender, but then they trapped and killed a number of soldiers once they entered the city. Hulugu was enraged and ordered a massacre of all the inhabitants of the caliphs' city. Some sources estimated, probably with some exaggeration, that this amounted to 300,000 men, women and children. Among those executed was the Abbasid caliph. Very few people escaped to tell the tale.

The Mongols came to rule over an empire which covered the Eurasian continent from the Caucasus Mountains to the China Sea. In the Muslim world, they dominated not only Iran, but also Iraq and parts of Syria and Anatolia. The Mamluk rulers of Egypt were the only Muslim force which succeeded in checking the Mongol advance at the battle of Ayn Jalut in 1260.

The Mongol's legacy was, however, much greater than the record of their conquests. The descendants of Chinggiz fulfilled in large measure his dream of creating a single world order. When the battles were over, the Mongols created an amazingly peaceful and stable empire. They encouraged trade and guarded the routes between West Asia, India and China. The famous European merchant-traveler Marco Polo easily traversed the distance between the Mediterranean coast and China. When he reached China, another grandson of Chinggiz, Kubilai Khan, took Marco into his service, showing that the Mongols had no fear of foreigners. The connection between the Mediterranean world and the regions farther to the East established by the Mongols was never entirely broken, even after their empire disappeared.

In time a more subtle transformation occurred which altered the character of the Mongol state. Oljaitu, the great-grandson of Chinggiz, accepted Islam. At the same time Persian culture began to dominate the rulers' courts. The Mongols intermarried with the local population, and in a few generations no one could distinguish them from their neighbors. Rather than being a threat to the Muslim world, the Mongols ended up being the guardians of Islamic faith and civilization.

A second wave of Turko-Mongol conquests occurred in the fourteenth century under the leadership of Timur-i Lang (Tamerlane). Timur was already a Muslim, but his attacks were in some ways even more destructive than those of Chinggiz's and Hulugu's time. After Timur's death, however, his empire rapidly disintegrated and his descendants came to rule over a small area of Central Asia. One of these, however, Zahir al-din Babar, went on to found the Mughal empire in India.

The Crusades

Pope Urban proclaimed the first Crusade in 1095 to rid the Holy Land from the "wicked Heathens." Ever since, the West has portrayed the two centuries of sporadic conflict as the forces of civilization against barbarians. In fact, the opposite was closer to the truth. Despite the political disunion, the cultural and scientific sophistication of the Arabs far exceeded that of the Crusaders.

Despite their superior level of learning and sophistication, the Abbasid Caliphs were too feeble to muster support for a real *jihad* and the Holy Land soon fell to the Franks.

Eventually, the Crusaders were forced out. The greatest Islamic victories came under Saladin (*Salah al-Din al-Ayubbi*). Saladin was ethnically a Kurd and *vizier* to the Caliph of Cairo. On the Caliph's death

Saladin made himself Sultan of Egypt. In 1187 he defeated the Crusaders and took control of the Levant and Palestine. The Europeans were left with just the coastal fortress cities of Antioch, Tripoli, and Tyre.

The third Crusade was then proclaimed against Saladin. Richard the Lion Heart, King of England, led the Crusaders in three years of inconclusive fighting against Saladin. The war ended in a truce that allowed pilgrims of all faiths access to their shrines in Jerusalem.

Saladin saved Islam with his victories and, by establishing an Islamic center of power at Cairo, kept it out of the hands of the Mongols.

IV
Islamic Empires in the Early Modern Period

The Turco-Mongol invasions and migrations were, as noted above, initially disruptive and destructive. Old state systems disappeared. The new ones were dominated by those steppe peoples. In time, first the Turkish speakers and eventually the Mongols became acclimated to the patterns of Islamic civilization. They accepted the Islamic faith and adopted Perso-Islamic cultural forms. Turks and Mongols became the founders of the three Islamic empires that dominated West and South Asia in the sixteenth, seventeenth, and early eighteenth centuries. Those empires were the Ottoman, Safavid, and Mughal.

The Ottomans

Seljuk Turks had been the first great Muslim empire builders who came from the steppe. While their kingdoms controlled parts of Syria and the Iranian plateau, another branch of the Seljuk family established itself in Anatolia. There, on the borders of the ever-shrinking Byzantine Empire, an unusual state came into being in the fourteenth and fifteenth centuries. Since the Byzantines called themselves the Romans, this Seljuk state was known throughout the Muslim world as *Rum,* an Arabicized version of "Rome." The Seljuk sultans of Rum fought a continual seesaw war with the Byzantines. The pressures created by this constant struggle meant that the kingdom of Rum was not as well organized as Seljuk states elsewhere in West Asia.

A melting pot The sultanate of Rum had a wild, frontier reputation. In part, this was caused by the war against the Byzantines. But it was also due partly to the kind of people attracted to or forced into a way of life centered on fighting. Anatolia became a dumping ground for individuals or groups who caused trouble for Seljuk rulers elsewhere. Rather than keep them close to the centers of civilization, sultans often ordered entire nomadic tribes to move to Rum where their energies could be employed in conquering the Byzantines. Other people came because they were attracted by the rough-and-ready world of the frontier warrior. These fighters known as *ghazi* (literally, "raiders") were supposed to be "holy warriors" fighting for the Islamic faith, trying to extend its dominion into Christian territory. In practice, many of them had their eyes on the chances a warrior kingdom offered to acquire loot and lay claim to conquered lands.

A few ambitious individuals probably hoped to be able to carve out their own states and make themselves kings. In the early 1300s, one of these petty princes, a leader of the Oghuz tribe of Turks, succeeded in creating a kingdom near the present city of Eskisehir (Turkey). His Islamic name "Uthman" was pronounced as "Osman" in Turkish. His followers took his name and Europeans later corrupted the pronunciation to "Ottoman."

Drive toward Constantinople In 1301, Osman's army defeated a Byzantine force at Baphaeon. This victory established Osman's kingdom as one of the major powers in Anatolia. Over the next one hundred and fifty years, under Osman's son, Orhan, and under Orhan's sons, the Ottomans gradually extended their hegemony further into Anatolia. In the process, they absorbed a number of other ghazi kingdoms while gradually, but continually, wearing down the Byzantines by snatching a bit of territory here and another bit there, always advancing toward Constantinople.

As part of their effort to encircle the Byzantines, the Ottomans crossed the Dardanelles to invade the Greek peninsula and the Balkans. The peoples living in the area now currently occupied by the modern states of Greece, Bulgaria, Albania, and Yugoslavia came from many different, mutually antagonistic ethnic or religious groups. They were unable to put up a unified defense of the region so that the Ottomans conquered them with comparative ease.

Constantinople, the ultimate objective of the Ottomans, was placed under siege in 1452. It fell after a tremendous battle in 1453 to the army of the sultan Mehmet II, known thereafter as "the Conqueror." The Ottomans immediately made the city their capital and declared themselves the Sultans of Rum.

In 1516, the Ottomans defeated the Mamluk rulers of Egypt and Syria, their only serious Muslim rivals in West Asia. The Ottomans learned much about the management of government by following the Mamluk example. Technically military slaves, the Mamluks had created one of the most highly centralized state systems in Muslim history. In addition, the Mamluks had succeeded in gaining the support and cooperation of large numbers of religious scholars.

After defeating the Mamluks, the Ottomans emptied their treasury in Cairo and sent it back to Istanbul (the Turkish pronunciation of Constantinople). They also took hundreds of thousands of documents from the Mamluk archives. They did this so that their own bureaucrats could imitate Mamluk procedures. Finally, they forced a number of Egyptian and Syrian religious scholars to move to Istanbul so that the Ottomans could use them to support their own imperial claims.

A long-lasting and diverse empire For more than three hundred years, the Ottomans controlled an empire that stretched from Hungary to the mountains of Armenia and from the Black Sea to the Arabian Peninsula. This vast territory was inhabited by dozens of different ethnic and religious groups. The Ottomans dealt with this diversity by allowing each religious group a certain amount of independence in the management of its internal affairs. These groups, or *millets* as the Ottomans called them, settled disputes among their own members, regulating such matters as marriage, divorce, and inheritance. They were also free to practice their religion so long as they did not try to convert Muslims. Until the First World War, the Ottomans were remarkably tolerant of non-Muslims so long as they did not foment rebellions.

One aspect of the Ottoman imperial system that excited a great deal of comment was their use of a corps of specially trained soldier-bureaucrats called in English, "Jannissaries," an English corruption of the Turkish words meaning "new soldier." The Janissaries were usually recruited from the rural Christian populations within the Ottoman Empire by a "man tax," the *devshirme,* which required the Christians to provide a certain number of boys as recruits for the ruling elite.

The anti-Ottoman feeling, which dominated European-American thought from the nineteenth century to the present, has turned the *devshirme* into a nightmare vision of terrible Turks (improperly referred to as dervishes) descending on poor Christian villagers in the dead of the night to kidnap helpless infant boys from the arms of their weeping mothers. As with most propaganda, the image did not come close to reality. The Ottoman officials responsible for the *devshirme* followed a regular, previously announced, schedule. The villagers knew when they were coming. They had ample opportunity to send into hiding those sons they wished to keep at home.

Frequently, those young men who became Janissaries did so because they or their parents wanted them to. The Janissaries provided not only the backbone of the Ottoman army, but also the chief administrators of the empire. Getting a post in this elite group gave a young man the opportunity for wealth and honor well above the ordinary expectations of a peasant. Far from being an "oriental despotism," the Ottoman state more closely resembled a modern "meritocracy" in which individuals gained admittance to a ruling elite and rose in its ranks on the basis of their abilities.

Like those of the Safavids and Mughals, the empire of the Ottomans provided the environment for an outpouring of literary and artistic genius. Poetry, not only in Turkish, but also in Persian, flourished under the Ottomans. Architects like the famous Sinan created buildings that have made Istanbul's skyline one of the world's most impressive sights. Painters, book binders, potters, glass blowers and bronze casters practiced their craft in a way that was seldom equaled and rarely surpassed.

The Safavids

In the wake of the Mongol invasions, various confederacies of nomadic and semi-nomadic peoples controlled what is now Iran. However, each of those coalitions maintained ties with the various cities and towns of the regions. There they traded the meat and skins of their herds for metal products and other manufactured goods. In addition, many of these towns were the headquarters for one or another Sufi order to which the nomads looked for spiritual guidance. The town of Ardabil near the west coast of the Caspian Sea was such a place. The tomb of a famous saint, Safi al-din, was located there.

Safi al-din's descendants, the Safavids, were the guardians of their holy ancestor's tomb as well as masters of the Sufi order which grew up around it. The Safavids of the late fourteenth century began to convert their spiritual authority into military and political power. They were able to weld the different Turkish tribes who attended the shrine into a powerful army. A young, charismatic leader of the Safavids,

Ismail, took advantage of this force to expand his control of areas quite distant from Ardabil. Ismail took on and defeated one of the major nomadic confederacies, the Aq-qoyunlu Turks. (Literally, *Aq-qoyunlu* means "the White Sheep." These Turks were so named because they hung the skins of white sheep on their banners.) Once he eliminated the leadership of this group, Ismail embarked on a series of campaigns which made him the master of most of what became contemporary Iran.

The Safavids were inclined to the Shiite branch of Islam. However, some of their religious beliefs were not exactly textbook versions of that faith. In his youth, Ismail had written poetry which indicated that he believed himself to be God incarnate. When his conquests were completed and he became the *Shahan Shah* (King of Kings), Ismail decided to bring his followers' beliefs into line with more sober versions of Shiism.

He invited Shiite religious scholars from the Persian Gulf and the mountains of Syria to take over the direction of religious affairs in his empire. This led to the ulama having more influence in Iran than in almost any other place in the Muslim world. While religious scholars usually refused to take a direct role in government, in the 1978-1979 Revolution in Iran, the ulama did use their unique authority to take a leading role in politics.

Shah Ismail made the Twelver branch of Shiism the religion of his court and sought to impose it upon the majority of his subjects. He sometimes forced conversions by violence or simply massacred Sunni dissidents. He took other steps to give stability to Safavid rule. He suppressed all other Sufi orders, perhaps fearing that some other Sufi leader would imitate his example. He found it necessary to purge the ranks of the tribal warriors who had brought him to the throne so that it would be impossible for them to put forward some other candidate. Finally, though Turkish was his mother tongue, Ismail aggressively pushed the cause of the Persian language and culture. Though many of those living in Iran continued to speak Turkish (today about one-third of Iranians), Persian acquired the prestige of being the court language.

In the sixteenth century, Iran presented a number of problems to any would-be empire builder. Many of its inhabitants were pastoral nomads. In order to control them, Ismail had to create alliances between himself and the chiefs of those tribal groups. He succeeded in making them loyal to the Safavid cause. Except for the regions close to the Caspian, Iran's peasant population lived in thousands of tiny hamlets scattered over the often inhospitable terrain of the plateau. Taking advantage of melting snow to provide moisture, many of these hamlets were in isolated mountain valleys. Direct rule of such a population would have been impossible. Ismail's only choice was to deal with the local strongmen who actually controlled the people of those regions. The alliances which Ismail formed worked remarkably well, and the Safavid dynasty survived until overthrown by a military adventurer in the eighteenth century.

The Safavid capital was moved several times—first from Ardabil to Tabriz, then from Tabriz to Qazvin, then to Isfahan. Each move put the Safavids closer to the geographical center of the Iranian plateau. It made it easier for the kings to administer the collection of tribute. It also put some distance between them and their major opponents, the Ottomans. The Ottomans had opposed Ismail's brutal suppression of Turkish-speaking Sunnis. They attacked the Safavids and defeated them on several occasions. Still, Ismail's alliances held firm and his successors eventually gained back most of what the Ottomans took.

Ismail's descendants were ardent patrons of all the Persian arts. The painters they sponsored created pictorial illustrations of books that set the standard followed elsewhere in the eastern Muslim world.

Likewise, the work of Iranian calligraphers was widely admired. Bookbinding and pottery-making also flourished. Some critics consider Iranian glazed tiles the most perfect expression of this art form. Shah Abbas I (1587–1629) made the city of Isfahan one of the most beautiful in the world. His architects designed and built palaces, mosques, madrasahs, and even bridges of tremendous beauty. Because of the Safavids, the citizens of the capital began to say with confidence, "Isfahan is half the world."

The Mughals

The Mughals were the last in a long line of invaders to arrive in India. From the year 1000 up to the middle of the nineteenth century, India was a frontier for the rest of the Muslim world. Like any frontier, it attracted the restless, the energetic, and those who needed a fresh environment in which to exercise their talents. Religiously, both Sunni and Shiah were present. Turks, Afghans, Arabs, Iranians, and Abyssinians were part of the ethnic mix of Muslim peoples in India.

Descent from the Turks The Mughals themselves were a hybrid people. As their name indicated (*Mughal* is the Persian word for Mongol), they were the progeny of Turco-Mongol empire-builders. Indeed, they claimed descent from Chinggiz Khan and Timur-i Lang (Tamerlane). Among themselves they spoke the Chagatai dialect of Turkish, but their court culture had been shaped in the Persianized cities of Central Asia. It was the loss of one of those cities, Ferghana, that drove an ambitious Mughal prince, Zahir al-Din, whose Mongol troops called him "Babar," meaning the "Panther," into India.

In 1526, Babar's small army defeated a much larger force led by the sultan of Delhi. In part, the victory was secured by Babar's use of field artillery imported from the Ottoman Empire, along with Turkish gunners to handle the weapons.

Babar died only four years after his initial victory. A rebellious governor forced Humayun, Babar's son, to spend some fifteen years in exile at the court of the Safavids. Humayun always had bad luck. Just six months after his return to India, he died after falling down a stairway. The real founder of the Mughal Empire, therefore, was Humayun's son Akbar (d. 1605). Only fourteen at the time of his father's death, Akbar was forced to accept the guidance of one of his father's advisers. At eighteen, he dismissed this minister and took the reins of power into his own hands.

Unlike the Safavids or Ottomans, the Mughals ruled over a territory in which the majority of the inhabitants were not Muslims. Over the centuries, Muslims were generally tolerant of Indian religions. As for the non-Muslims, many of them cooperated with the Muslim rulers, imitated their styles of dress, learned Persian, and even rose to positions of authority in the army and administration. Thus, Akbar was able to draw on centuries of experience in shaping a governmental system that drew together Muslims and non-Muslims.

Akbar, like most other pre-modern rulers, faced the problem of controlling a huge territory with agents who were often tempted to assert their independence from the emperor. Akbar devised a system of awarding ranks, called *mansabs,* to all his officials. Known as *mansabdars* (rank holders), these men commanded the armies, governed the provinces, acted as accountants, and also formed the empire's nobility. In order to oversee the work of the mansabdars, Akbar established the principle that the emperor should personally admit, promote, demote, or punish all high-ranking officers. A post in the imperial nobility could not be inherited. As a result, many talented individuals, both Muslims and non-Muslims, gained entry into the imperial service.

Akbar's arrangements worked so well that the next three emperors, Jahangir (d. 1627), Shah Jahan (d. 1658) and Alamgir, also known as Aurangzeb (d. 1707) succeeded in preserving the empire and expanding it until, in the reign of Aurangzeb, it claimed dominion over the whole of India and parts of Afghanistan as well.

Over the period between 1526 and 1739, the Mughal name acquired such prestige that even after the emperors lost all their power, their would-be successors tried to gain imperial approval for their actions. Even the British, who became Indian empire-builders in their own right, made their conquests in the name of the Mughals.

Mughal legacy The excellence of the arts of the Mughal period also became legendary. In architecture, mosques and tombs put up under Mughal patronage were among the world's most impressive buildings. The Taj Mahal was the most famous of them, but it was only one among dozens of others located throughout the subcontinent. Art historians have long considered Mughal era paintings some of the most interesting in the world. Since Persian was the language of the Mughal government, the incentive to learn it as well as compose prose and poetry in it was strong. Even in its decline, Mughal authors and artists managed to maintain a high level of excellence.

Empires in Decline

A few European travelers and merchants visited Ottoman, Safavid, and Mughal territories when these empires were at the height of their wealth and influence. They were much impressed by what they saw. The title by which Europeans referred to them,

"The Grand Turk," "The Great Sofie (Sufi)," and "The Great Mogul," testified to the awe that those three Muslim empires inspired. In English, the word "mogul" still describes someone who possesses money and power. Such things should remind us that Asian Muslim empires were larger and more powerful than any of the European nations.

European threats By the eighteenth century, however, when Europeans came in greater numbers and when they came armed to the teeth, these empires were already beginning to show signs of collapse. A military adventurer overthrew the Safavid dynasty in 1722. After the death of Aurangzeb in 1707, the Mughal Empire began to break up. At about the same time, the Ottoman Empire experienced a serious threat from an expanding Russian empire. Over the next two hundred years, external pressure combined with internal rebellions placed the central administration under severe stress.

The decline of these empires was, in part, the result of an aging process common to pre-modern states. The Mughals and Ottomans controlled vast territories. In the days before modern communications, that was in itself a serious weakness. In addition, empires like these flourished only when they expanded. The resources that new conquests provided gave them the ability to attract and hold the support of influential local leaders. At the beginning of the eighteenth century, both the Ottoman and Mughal empires had reached their farthest limits. The wealthy and powerful in each were forced to turn inward, placing maximum demands on ever more limited reserves.

European intrusion or internal revolt only added to the difficulties they faced in surviving. While the Europeans contributed to the decline of the early modern Muslim empires, they were in a position to take greater advantage of their losses. That the nations of Europe grew more prosperous and powerful, while those of Muslim Asia grew poorer, exerted great influence on Euro-American perceptions of the Muslim world. Part of the contempt, which they often expressed for Muslims, was rooted in this temporary superiority they enjoyed over enfeebled Muslim states. Though the Muslim world began to recover in the nineteenth and twentieth centuries, Euro-American attitudes have largely remained in an eighteenth century intellectual universe, in which the Muslim world deserved little attention.

Westernization

From North Africa to the Indonesian archipelago, the Islamic world had become so poor and backward it was no match for the European ascendancy of the 1900s.

The local ruling elites first fell into quasi-colonial submission and eventually to outright imitation of European commercial and legal practices, mannerisms, forms and culture.

The dissolution of the Ottoman Empire following its defeat in World War I, and the imposition of protectorates, artificial nation states and borders, resulted in political turmoil and wars that continue to this day.

Compounding the post-colonial problems in the nations of Islam is the continuing and centuries-old tension between the secular authority and the religious. Although separation of church and state is accepted as the norm in the West, it is not so in Islamic countries.

The Islamic world has now, on one extreme, Turkey. For three generations it has been a secular state westernized even to the abandonment of Arabic script. On the other extreme is Iran, which under the Ayatollah Khomeini, at least, was nearly a pure theocracy. Between the two extremes, each of the remaining Muslim nations seeks its own particular balance.

The political and economic systems that this quest for balance has engendered are so different that rivalry and tension between them are the rule, rather than the Islamic ideal of unity, which is still revered and fervently sought.

V
Islam: World Faith, Political System, and Civilizational Tradition

There are no convenient boundaries that define the world of Islam. The religious movement had its roots in the Arabian Peninsula, but it soon spread throughout West, South, and Southeast Asia. Though the Arabic language still has an important place, because it is the language of sacred scripture and theology, it is not the mother-tongue of the vast majority of the world's 800 million Muslims. Something less than one-third of that total are Arabic-speakers. The largest concentrations of Muslims are found in southeastern and southern Asia. Indonesia has some 125 million Muslim inhabitants, which makes it the largest single Muslim nation. It is followed by Bangladesh (eastern Bengal) which has 88 million Muslims, then India with some 80 million and Pakistan with 77 million. Perhaps 100 million Muslims live in the Soviet Socialist Republics of Uzbekistan, Azerbaijan, Kurdistan, Tajikstan, and other Soviet republics. A similar number are living in the northwestern provinces of the People's Republic of China. Moreover, Islam continues to make converts in Africa, Thailand, Burma, and even in Europe and America. Islam's ability to attract and hold new adherents makes it the world's fastest-growing religious faith.

In the readings that follow, it is possible to give only a hint of the many diverse aspects of Muslim history. The first readings deal with Islam as a religious faith. They are taken from the *Holy Quran,* the written revelation of the faith. The second section deals with the political vision that is part of Islam's idealistic view of the world. It also reports on the practical compromises that have been made in creating political institutions. Finally, the last section deals with some aspects of civilization that Muslims created.

The *Holy Quran*

Theme I: The Piety of Ethical Monotheism

According to Islamic doctrine, the *Holy Quran* is a direct copy of God's own book which exists in heaven. This book was gradually revealed to the Prophet Muhammad by the Angel Gabriel. Muhammad recited (the literal meaning of the Arabic word, *Qur'an*) the revelations that the angel brought him. Throughout the years of his active ministry, roughly A.D. 610–632, the Prophet received and transmitted many separate revelations. When these were pronounced, the messages were sometimes memorized by those who heard them and sometimes they were written down. Within twenty years of the Prophet's death (A.D. 632), a written copy of all the revelations was collated. The text was corrected by comparing whatever written records there were and by consulting those who had actually heard the revelations spoken. Each revelation was considered as a separate *surah*, or chapter. Except for the first surah, known as the *fatihah*, "The Opening," the chapters were arranged from longest to shortest. Each of the *Quran*'s surahs contains several different kinds of material. Revelations concerning the spirit of piety that believers should have are mixed with those governing personal and social behavior. Each of these should be looked upon as a distinct element. Therefore, the selections that follow are arranged thematically, with different verses taken from a number of surahs.

The *Quran* Interpreted

Surah I: The *Fatihah*, "The Opening." It is also sometimes known as "The Essence of the *Quran*."

In the name of Allah (God), the
        Beneficent, the
Merciful.
        Praise be to Allah, Lord of the Worlds,
        The Beneficent, the Merciful.
        The Master of the Day of Judgment,
        You alone we worship; You alone we
            ask for aid.
        Show us the right path,
        The way taken by those that You love.
        Lead us not on the path of those who
            anger You, nor of those who lose
            their way.

By custom each Surah is known by a common "nickname," which refers to some prominent theme or character in the *surah*. The following verses are taken from the Fourth surah, commonly known as "The Women" because much of it has to do with the rights and duties of females. However, there are many other themes introduced, such as the pious sentiments that follow.

        To God belongs all that is in the heavens
            and in the earth.
        We have charged those who were given
            the Book before you, and you, 'Fear
            God.'
        If you disbelieve, to God belongs all that is
            in the heavens and in the earth; God
            is All-sufficient, All-laudable.
        To God belongs all that is in the heavens
            and in the earth; God suffices for a
            guardian.
        If He will, He can put you away, O men,
            and bring others; surely God is
            powerful over that.

Whoso desires the reward of this world,
  with God is the reward of this world
  and of the world to come; God is All-
  hearing, All-seeing.
O believers, believe in God and His
  Messenger and the Book He has sent
  down on His Messenger and the
  Book which he sent down before.
Whoso disbelieves in God and His angels
  and His Books, and His Messengers,
  and the Last Day, has surely gone
  astray into far error.
Those who believe, and then disbelieve,
  and then believe, and then
  disbelieve, and then increase in
  unbelief—God is not likely to forgive
  them, neither to guide them on any
  way
. . . recite of it so much as is feasible.
And perform the prayer, and pay the
  alms, and lend to God a good loan.
Whatever good you shall forward to your
  souls' account, you shall find it with
  God as better, and mightier a wage.
And ask God's forgiveness; God is All-
  forgiving, All-compassionate.

Human beings are expected to behave according to
God's commands for two reasons. Partly because
avoiding the evil and seeking the good is something
inherently worthwhile, but also because God will
punish those who do evil and reward those who do
good. The following verses taken from the Fourth
Surah illustrate the point.

And whosoever does deeds of
  righteousness, be it male or female,
  believing—they shall enter Paradise,

and not be wronged a single date-spot.

And who is there that has a fairer religion than he who submits his will to God being a good-doer, and who follows the creed of Abraham, a man of pure faith?

And God took Abraham for a friend.

To God belongs all that is in the heavens and in the earth, and God encompasses everything.

Those are God's bounds. Whoso obeys God and His Messenger, He will admit him to gardens underneath which rivers flow, therein dwelling forever; that is the mighty triumph.

But whoso disobeys God, and His Messenger, and transgresses His bounds, him He will admit to a Fire, therein dwelling forever, and for him there awaits a humbling chastisement.

Hast thou not regarded those who were given a share of the Books believing in demons and idols, and saying to the unbelievers, These are more rightly guided on the way than the believers?

Those are they whom God has cursed; he whom God has cursed, thou wilt not find for him any helper.

Or have they a share in the Kingdom? If that is so, they do not give the people a single date-spot.

Or are they jealous of the people for the bounty that God has given them?

Yet we gave the people of Abraham the
 Book and the Wisdom, and We gave
 them a mighty kingdom.
And some of them there are that believe,
 and some of them that are far from
 it; Gehenna suffices for a Blaze!

Surely those who disbelieve in Our
 signs—We shall certainly roast them
 as a Fire; as often as their skins are
 wholly burned, We shall give them
 in exchange other skins, that they
 may taste the chastisement.
Surely God is All-mighty, All-wise. And
 those that believe, and do deeds of
 righteousness, them We shall admit
 to gardens underneath which rivers
 flow, therein dwelling forever and
 ever; therein shall be spouses
 purified, and We shall admit them
 to a shelter of plenteous shade.

As the contrasting images of the Garden of Paradise
and the flames of Hell make the believer desire the
one and fear the other, the image of Judgment Day is
intended to remind the believer that this world will be
destroyed one day and it is better to think of the next
world before becoming too attached to this one. For
instance, the following verses from the Seventy-fifth
Surah call up the images of the "Day of Wrath.."

But when the sight is dazed
and the moon is eclipsed,
and the sun and moon are brought
 together,
upon that day man shall say, 'Whither to
 flee?'
No indeed; not a refuge!

Upon that day the recourse shall be to thy
   Lord.
Upon that day man shall be told his
   former deeds and his latter;
nay, man shall be a clear proof against
   himself,
even though he offer his excuses.

Theme II: The Prophet Muhammad and the Prophets Who Came Before Him

In the nineteenth century, it was fashionable to refer to Islam as Muhammadism and to its adherents as Muhammadans. This was actually an insult to Muslims. According to Muslim teaching, the Prophet Muhammad was not the founder of a new religion. Islam was the first religion of humanity. Adam, the first man, was also the Prophet of Islam. Though it was the natural religion of humankind, it was sometimes ignored or rejected. Therefore, it was necessary for God to send the prophets who called people to return to the path.

The following selections from the Fourth Surah speak of Muhammad's relationship to all the preceding prophets.

Because each of the prophets brought a copy of the heavenly book, Christians, Jews, and sometimes Zoroastrians are known as "People of the Book." Although the Hebrew Bible (Torah) and the Gospel became hopelessly corrupted, the Christians and Jews were still entitled to protection and tolerance, for they once possessed a true copy of God's book.

The People of the Book will ask thee to
   bring down upon them a Book from
   heaven; and they asked Moses for
   greater than that, for they said,
   "Show us God openly."

And the thunderbolt took them for their
     evildoing. Then they took to
     themselves the Calf, after the clear
     signs had come to them; yet We
     pardoned them that, and We
     bestowed upon Moses a clear
     authority.
And We raised above them the Mount,
     taking compact with them; and We
     said to them, "Transgress not the
     Sabbath"; and We took from them a
     solemn compact.
So, for their breaking the compact, and
     disbelieving in the signs of God, and
     slaying the Prophets without right,
     and for their saying, 'Our hearts are
     circumcised'—nay, but God sealed
     them for their unbelief, so they
     believe not, except a few—and for
     their unbelief, and their uttering
     against Mary a mighty calumny, and
     for their saying, 'We slew the
     Messiah, Jesus son of Mary, the
     Messenger of God'—yet they did not
     slay him, neither crucified him, only
     a likeness of that was shown to
     them.
Those who are at variance concerning
     him surely are in doubt regarding
     him; they have no knowledge of
     him, except the following of surmise;
     and they slew him not of a
     certainty—no indeed; God raised
     him up to Him; God is All-mighty,
     All-wise.
There is not one of the People of the Book
     but will assuredly believe in him

before his death, and on the
Resurrection Day he will be a witness
against them.

And for the evildoing of those of Jewry,
We have forbidden them certain
good things that were permitted to
them, and for their barring from
God's way many, and for their taking
usury, that they were prohibited, and
consuming the wealth of the people
in vanity; and We have prepared for
the unbelievers among them a
painful chastisement.

We have revealed to thee as We revealed
to Noah, and the Prophets after him,
and We revealed to Abraham,
Ishmael, Isaac, Jacob, and the Tribes,
Jesus and Job, Jonah and Aaron and
Solomon, and We gave to David
Psalms.

People of the Book, go not beyond the
bounds in your religion, and say not
as to God but the truth.

The Messiah, Jesus son of Mary was only
the Messenger of God, and His Word
that HE committed to Mary, and a
Spirit from Him.

So believe in God and His Messengers,
and say not, 'Three.'

Refrain; better is it for you.

God is only One God.

Glory be to Him—that He should have a
son!

To Him belongs all that is in the heavens
and in the earth; God suffices for a
guardian.

The Messiah will not disdain to be a
   servant of God, neither the angels
   who are near stationed to Him.
Whosoever disdains to serve Him, and
   waxes proud, He will assuredly
   muster them to Him, all of them.
As for the believers, who do deeds of
   righteousness, He will pay them in
   full their wages, and He will give
   them more, of His bounty; and as for
   them who disdain, and wax proud,
   them He will chastise with a painful
   chastisement, and they shall not find
   for them, apart from God, a friend or
   helper.
O men, a proof has now come to you
   from your Lord; We have sent down
   to you a manifest light.
The Messiah will not disdain to be a
   servant.

Theme III: Social Justice and Behavior

Within the tradition of ethical monotheism there
has always been a great concern for social justice. The
belief that God wished people to be honest with all was
found among the prophets of the Hebrew Bible and in
the teachings of Jesus. In the *Quran* the command to
deal fairly and to be kind was often repeated. Also, in
the *Quran* one finds this concern for justice translated
into specific guidelines for behavior. For instance, in
the verse that follows, we find not only demands for
justice, but we see actual prescriptions on how to
practice it. In a long section of the verse we find the
proportions assigned to family members in
inheritance. Such rules were intended to protect an
individual's dependents. Though the shares were not
equal, the rules were designed to see to it that everyone
got something from the dead person's estate. Modern

Muslim commentators also explain the command to divide property as a way of ensuring social equality by preventing the accumulation of vast estates. Although women were not granted a share equal to that of males, women had been completely ignored before the revelation brought by Muhammad.

Islam claims to be a total system of life. There is nothing in life, private or public, that is not part of its teaching. Therefore, the *Quran* addresses itself to such topics as the relationship of husband and wife. It insists that business contracts be completely fulfilled. The *Quran* includes prescriptions for diet. For instance, it forbids the drinking of wine or the eating of pork. I develops the notion of ritual purity. It describes those substances that are impure, such as urine, feces, blood, dead bodies, and those acts, such as sexual intercourse that make a person ritually impure. Before praying, it insists that individuals wash or, if there is no water handy, make use of clean sand to purify themselves. Much of the *Quran* is taken up with informing man of what God expects, "So that man can have no argument with God."

> Give the orphans their property, and do
> > not exchange the corrupt for the
> > good; and devour not their property
> > with your property; surely that is a
> > great crime.
> If you fear that you will not act justly
> > towards the orphans, marry such
> > women as seem good to you, two,
> > three, four; but if you fear you will
> > not be equitable, then only one, or
> > what your right hands own so it is
> > likelier you will not be partial.
> And give the women their dowries as a
> > gift spontaneous; but if they are
> > pleased to offer you any of it,

consume it with wholesome
appetite.
But do not give to fools their property
that God has assigned to you to
manage; provide for them and clothe
them out of it, and speak to them
honourable words.
Test well the orphans, until they reach
the age of marrying; then, if you
perceive in them right judgment,
deliver to them their property;
consume it not wastefully and
hastily ere they are grown.
If any man is rich, let him be abstinent; if
poor, let him consume in reason.
And when you deliver to them their
property, take witnesses over them;
God suffices for a reckoner.

O believers, be you securers of justice,
witnesses for God, even though it be
against yourselves, or your parents
and kinsmen, whether the man be
rich or poor; God stands closest to
either.
Then follow not caprice, so as to swerve;
for you twist or turn, God is aware of
the things you do.

God commands you to deliver trusts back
to their owners; and when you judge
between the people, that you judge
with justice.
Good is the admonition God gives you;
God is All-hearing, All-seeing.
Serve God, and associate naught with
Him.
Be kind to parents, and the near kinsman,
and to orphans, and to the needy,

and the neighbour who is of kin, and
to the neighbour who is a stranger,
and to the companion at your side,
and to the traveller, and to that your
right hands own.
Surely God loves not the proud and
boastful such as are niggardly, and
bid other men to be niggardly, and
themselves conceal the bounty that
God has given them.
We have prepared for the unbelievers a
humbling chastisement, and such as
expend of their substance to show off
to men, and believe not in God and
the Last Day.
Whosoever has Satan for a comrade, an
evil comrade is he.
Why, what would it harm them, if they
believed in God and the Last Day,
and expended of that God has
provided them?
God knows them.
O believers, consume not your goods
between you in vanity, except there
be trading, by your agreeing together.
And kill not one another.
Surely God is compassionate to you.
But whosoever does that in transgression
and wrongfully, him We shall
certainly roast at a Fire; and that for
God is an easy matter.
If you avoid the heinous sins that are
forbidden you, We will acquit you by
the gate of honour.

To the men a share of what parents and
kinsmen leave, and to the women a
share of what parents and kinsmen

leave, whether it be little or much, a share apportioned; and when the division is attended by kinsmen and orphans of the poor, make provision for them out of it, and speak to them honourable words.

And let those fear who, if they left behind them weak seed, would be afraid on their account, and let them fear God, and speak words hitting the mark.

Those who devour the property of orphans unjustly, devour Fire in their bellies, and shall assuredly roast in a Blaze.

God charges you, concerning your children: to the male the like of the portion of two females, and if they be women above two, then for them two-thirds of what he leaves, but if she be one then to her a half; and to his parents to each one of the two the sixth of what he leaves, if he has children; but if he has no children, and his heirs are his parents, a third to his mother, or, if he has brothers, to his mother a sixth, after any bequest he may bequeath, or any debt.

Your fathers and your sons—you know not which out of them is nearer in profit to you. So God apportions; surely God is All-knowing, All-wise.

Men are the managers of the affairs of women for that God has preferred in bounty one of them obey another, and for that they have expended of their property.

Righteous women are therefore obedient,
    guarding the secret for God's
    guarding.
And those you fear may be rebellious
    admonish; banish them to their
    couches, and beat them.
If they then obey you, look not for any
    way against them; God is All-high,
    All-great.
And if you fear a breach between the two,
    bring forth an arbiter from his people
    and from her people an arbiter, if
    they desire to set things right; God
    will compose their differences; surely
    God is All-knowing, All-aware.
O Prophet, when you divorce women,
    divorce them when they have
    reached their period. Count the
    period, and fear God your lord. Do
    not expel them from their houses,
    nor let them go forth, except when
    they commit a flagrant indecency.
Those are God's bounds; whosoever
    trespasses the bounds of God has
    done wrong to himself.
Thou knowest not, perchance after that
    God will bring something new to
    pass.
Then, when they have reached their
    term, retain them honourably, or
    part from them honourably.
And call in to witness two men of equity
    from among yourselves; and
    perform the witnessing to God
    Himself.
By this then is admonished whosoever
    believes in God and the Last Day.

And whosoever fears God, He will
appoint for him a way out, and He
will provide for him from whence
he never reckoned.

As for your women who are despaired of
further menstruating, if you are in
doubt, their period shall be three
months, and those who have not
menstruated as yet.
And those who are with child, their term
is when they bring forth their
burden.
Whoso fears God, God will appoint for
him, of His command, easiness.

O believers, draw not near to prayer when
you are drunken until you know
what you are saying, or defiled—
unless you are traversing a way—
until you have washed yourselves;
but if you are sick, or on journey, of
if any of you comes from the privy,
or you have touched women, and
you can find no water, then have
recourse to wholesome dust and
wipe your faces and your hands; God
is All-pardoning, All-forgiving.

The Expansion of Islam

The Western world retains the popular image of
Islamic armies rampaging fanatically across many
countries, killing and destroying and forcing everyone
to convert to the new religion or perish. In fact,
Muslims in these campaigns were no more
bloodthirsty than any other military force, and their
treatment of conquered cities and peoples was often
quite a lot better. Conquered people were not forced to
convert to Islam, and were in fact protected and

defended so long as they did not rebel against their new rulers or aid those who might rebel. In addition, non-believers had to pay a special tax, called a *jizya*, but no other burdens were placed on them. In all, Muslims treated their defeated enemy with far greater respect for their religion, property, and persons than most other victors would have. We need only recall the result of the European Crusaders' capture of Jerusalem in 1099, when more than 100,000 Muslims, Jews, and Christians in the city were slaughtered in cold blood, to recognize the mildness of the early days of Islam's rule over those of other faiths.

Reprinted here are translations of peace treaties imposed by Muslim conquerors on some of the countries and cities they captured, including Jerusalem. Notice that the Muslims agree not only to refrain from converting or looting their subjects, but agree to actually protect them from other threats as long as they do not rebel against their new rulers.

Bánqiyá and Barmá (633)

In the name of God, the Merciful and the Compassionate.

This is a letter from Khálid ibn al-Walid to Salúba ibn Nastúná and his people.

I have made a pact with you for *jizya* and defense for every fit man, for both Bánqiyá and Barmá, for 10,000 dinars, excluding coins with holes punched in them, the wealthy according to the measure of his wealth, the poor according to the measure of his poverty, payable annually. You have been made head of your people and your people are content with you. I, therefore, and the Muslims who are with me, accept you, and I and your people are content. You have protection (*dhimma*) and defense. If we defend you, the *jizya* is due to us; if we do not, it is not, until we do defend you.

Witnessed by Hishám ibn al-Walid, al-Qaqá ibn Amr, Jarir ibn Abdalláh al Himyarí and Hanzala ibn al-Rabí.

Written in the year 12, in *Safar* (April–May 633).
Al-Tabarí, i, 2050.

Jerusalem (636)

In the name of God the Merciful and the Compassionate.

This is the safe-conduct accorded by the servant of God Umar, the Commander of the Faithful, to the people of Aelia [Jerusalem].

He accords them safe-conduct for their persons, their property, their churches, their crosses, their sound and their sick, and the rest of their worship.

Their churches shall neither be used as dwellings nor destroyed. They shall not suffer any impairment, nor shall their dependencies, their crosses, nor any of their property.

No constraint shall be exercised against them in religion nor shall any harm be done to any among them.

No Jew shall live with them in Aelia.

The people of Aelia must pay the *jizya* in the same way as the people of other cities.

They must expel the Romans and the brigands from the city. Those who leave shall have safe-conduct for their persons and property until they reach safety. Those who stay shall have safe-conduct and must pay the *jizya* like the people of Aelia.

Those of the people of Aelia who wish to remove their persons and effects and depart with the Romans and abandon their churches and their crosses shall have safe-conduct for their persons, their churches, and their crosses, until they reach safety.

The country people who were already in the city before the killing of so-and-so may, as they wish, remain and pay the *jizya* the same way as the people of Aelia or leave with the Romans or return to their families. Nothing shall be taken from them until they have gathered their harvest.

This document is placed under the surety of God and the protection [*dhimma*] of the Prophet, the Caliphs and the believers, on condition that the inhabitants of Aelia pay the *jizya* that is due from them.

Witnessed by Khalid ibn al-Walid, Amr ibn al-As, Abdal-Rahmán ibn Awf, Muáwiya ibn Abí Sufya, the last of whom wrote this document in the year 15 [636]. Al-Tabarí, i, 2405–4206.

Adharbayján (639)

In the name of God, the Merciful and the Compassionate.

This is what Utba ibn Farqad, governor for Umar ibn al-Khattáb, Commander of the Faithful, gave to the inhabitants of Adharbayján, its plains and hills and dependencies and borderlands and all the people of its communities: Safe-conduct for themselves, their property, their religions, and their laws, on the condition that they pay the jizya according to their capacity, but not for the child or the woman or for the sick or the pious hermit, who owns nothing of the goods of this world. This is for them and for whoever dwells with them. Their obligation is to lodge any Muslim from the Muslim armies for a day and a night and to guide him. If anyone of them dies in a year, he is relieved of the *jizya* for that year. If anyone stays [with them] he is in the same position as they are [that is, as regards obligations and rights]; if anyone goes forth, he has safe-conduct until he reaches safety.

Written by Jundub and witnessed by Bukayr ibn Abdalláh al Laythí and Simák ibn Kharasha al-Ansárí.

Written in 18 [639]
Al-Tabarí, i, 2662.

Islam as a Political System

Political realities and the demands of religion sometimes came into conflict. Even though rulers were sometimes corrupt and believing men compromised with them, the vision of a perfect Islamic political order remained part of the teaching of the faith. The idea that the state should encourage justice, charity, and piety has sparked many religio-social rebellions in the Muslim world. Today the ideal still remains a potent idea, if not a reality, for many Muslims.

The readings that follow represent the works of one man who wished to see the state guided by the teachings of Islam and another who felt that some compromise between the ideal and the real had to be made.

From *The Mauizah-yi-Jahangiri* by Baqir Khan, composed in the first half of the seventeenth century:

> It is absolutely necessary that there shall be that chosen being of creation called a king. In the days after the Prophet Muhammad (on whom be God's peace and blessings), who was the last prophet, kings were necessary so that the fundamentals of the faith be proclaimed and enforced. (Kings see to it) That the actions of men are correct and their well-being protected. A single lord and ruler guarantees that there will be peace and prosperity. A king should be a man worthy of imitation. He should possess tremendous power, but the power should be used to secure justice.
>
> By using the power, but avoiding the warrior's anger, man's animal passions will be avoided. People will be taught to remember the Prophets and their teachings. They will forget their own evil desires. They will not be overwhelmed by lust, nor give in to frivolous ways.

(United under one King) They will not be consumed in a struggle for dominance over each other.

A king should have the morals of a man who is learned in the way of the faith. All his conduct should have its foundation in the rules of faith. Following this path will make his rule as splendid as the kingly robes· he wears. The king should expend all his powers toward learning what the men of faith (the *ulama*) make known to him. Their guidance, their opinions should be the source of the king's policy. In this way, the king will receive the crown of success. His kingdom and its subjects will be happy, well-fed, content, obedient and loyal, his name will be famous throughout time.

From the *Fatáwai Jahandárí* (Opinions of those who rule the World) composed by Zia al-Din Barni in the mid-fourteenth century A.D.

Kings would not be able to rule their subjects if they did not have power, or if they did not remind men of that power through a display of wealth. Only in the time of the first four, rightly guided, *Khalifahs* did rulers live frugal lives. Although they subjugated the world, they were humble and just. This was possible because at that time the memory of the Holy Prophet and his deeds was strong. But those days were an exceptional time. Those *Khalifahs* lived according to the example of the Prophet. If kings in our day tried to do the same, they would soon lose their thrones . . . Never again will kings and princes be able to rule as the first *Khalifahs* did. The *Khalifahs* were the leaders of men who respected the Prophet and his teachings. In our day, the world is full of men who are like animals . . .

Today there are only a few people who firmly believe and truly practice the faith of Islam. People are content to make a vain display of their faith, but, in truth, they seek the good things of this world. In our day, they are beginning to take the same path. No king can expect obedience, nor can he vanquish his enemies, if he lives a life both poor and pious. If a king will not force men to obey, they will act like savages. They will eat each other alive. No one will follow the orders of governors and officials. There will be rebellion daily and daily repression. The chaos of former days will return. . .

And so, after the first *Khalifahs*, Muslim kings began to copy the ways of the *Shahs* of Persia. They dressed like them. They ate like them. Like the *Shahs*, they destroyed all who rebelled and crushed all who were presumptuous. In doing that, they sometimes did not follow the precepts of the Prophet. But, if the Prophet is the paragon of the true faith, the Shah is the paragon of temporal prosperity. In the way they live, in their aims, the two are opposed. There is no practical way to combine both.

So, oh sons of the Prophet, be aware that one can not be a king without adopting the ways of the Persian Shahs. All those who are learned in the faith (the *ulama*) know well that those customs contradict the practice of the Prophet and the ways of the faith.

Islam as a Civilizational System

Islamic civilization, like all other civilizational traditions, blended several different cultural traditions. Two important cultural strands had their origin in the Arabian Peninsula. Although the Prophet and his first followers were town-dwelling merchants, the Arabs of the seventh century A.D. were still under the influence of their nomadic cousins. The Arabs who lived in the desert, the Bedouin (Arabic: *Badawi*) took delight in war and romance. In pre-Islamic, Arabic poetry these traditions of personal courage and eroticism were preserved, sometimes to the exclusion of the more sober and puritanical Islamic strain. Because of the importance of the *Quran*, which was transmitted in the Arabic language, and also because of the initial importance of Arab culture, these forms were transmitted to many non-Arabs who embraced the faith. In the literatures of languages as diverse as Turkish and Malay, one finds not only Arabic words, but also themes and values which had their origin in the cultures of the first Muslims.

Another component in this mixing of traditions was provided by the heritage of many centuries of Iranian civilization. Ideas about the person and functions of kings, bureaucratic government and dynastic succession were one visible legacy from Iran's past. The Persian language also gave new literary forms such as elegant prose and epic poetry. Iranians also played a crucial role in the development of Islamic mysticism: Sufism.

A third major contribution to Islamic civilization was made by Hellenism, which had its roots in the conquests of Alexander the Great (c. 330 B.C.) Alexander's conquests made possible a synthesis between the classical Greek tradition and the traditions of Western Asia. That synthesis was Hellenism. The Romans preserved and extended these cultural forms. Hellenism also influenced the development of Christian thought. When the Arabs entered the area, the Christians of Syria and Byzantium as well as the Persians still preserved Hellenism. Muslims also fell under the spell of its traditions. In science, mathematics, philosophy, and logic, the Hellenistic thinkers of Western Asia served the Muslims as teachers. The most visible contribution of Hellenism was in Islamic architecture. Muslim builders quickly began using arches and columns as the Romans had.

It is impossible to present examples of all the different aspects of the Islamic civilizational tradition. In the following selections we have first some poetry translated from the Arabic, Persian, and Urdu (the national language of Pakistan) languages. Also, we provide two selections that illustrate the comparative superiority of Islamic civilization to that of Europe during the period we call the "Middle Ages."

The following poem is an example of pre-Islamic poetry. Its blending of sexuality and threatened violence was characteristic of the nomad's style.

> She was fair to behold, but she was
>   covered with veils and closely
>   guarded.
> Yet, when I stole into her tent, she
>   welcomed me with open arms.
> Though her brothers would have
>   murdered me, I passed through the
>   tent ropes.

I appeared at midnight when the stars
were thick in the sky.
Alone in her tent she had cast off her
many veils and wore only her night
dress.
"Are you mad?" she asked me when she
first saw me.
"My brothers will kill you."
But we left her tent and hurried to the
desert and lay down in the sand.
Beyond the watch fires and far from
suspicious eyes, we lay, where none
save us could see.
Her dark tresses encircled me as I drew
her face to mine.
Her waist was as thin as the ankle rings
she wore.
Her face was fair without a hint of red.
Her breasts were as smooth as glass.
She became mine.

As the Islamic Empire spread, the way of life of the
Arabs changed quickly as they adopted the lifestyle of
the people they conquered. Even so, there was some
nostalgia for the old ways of the desert. The following
poem was written in the eighth century A.D. by a
woman who was a khalifah's wife.

I would prefer a tent in the desert to these
great marble halls.
A simple wool cloak I would take instead
of shimmering silk.
I would rather eat a crust of bread than
feast every day on dainty pastries.
Around me I would have hunting dogs
that bark, not cats that slyly smile.
To fall asleep to the music of the wind is
better than to doze while tamborines
jingle.

A young man's daring I wish for, not my
        husband's coy romancing.
I love the rude, half-starved desert man,
        not princes grown fat and slow.

As noted above, the spirit of Muslim poetry often
was in conflict with the strict morality that Islam
preached and that Muslims sometimes practiced.

The truly pious man was often a figure of fun. The
following poem is an example. It was written in the
eighteenth century by a Muslim living in India.

If there were wine and privacy and the
        fair-face of one's beloved, Oh! Puritan!
swear an oath, if you were there, what
        would you do?

As with other poetry, Muslim poetry tells of the
pains of life and love. It recalls moments spent in
drunken frolic and hours spent in guilt and remorse.
The religious mystics of Islam, the *Sufis*, often used
such poetry as a vehicle for their teaching. Verses that
praised the drinking of wine (something forbidden in
the *Quran*) or physical love were reinterpreted by the
mystics. Wine became a metaphor for divine love. The
exhilaration of alcohol became a way of expressing the
exhilaration of God's love. Love poetry was also
reinterpreted and the human lover was used as a
symbol for God.

The following poem by the Persian poet Omar
Khayyám who lived in the tenth century A.D., reflects
a kind of skepticism often found in Persian poetry.

When I was a child, I sometimes went to
        a teacher.
And sometimes I taught myself, but
        eventually I learned
The limits to all knowledge: we come into
        this world upon
the waters, we leave it on the wind.

The following poems are taken from a number of poets writing in India in the nineteenth century. They include Bahadur Shah Zafar, the last Mughal emperor who died in 1862 and Mirza Asad-ullah Khan Ghalib, who is acknowledged as the greatest poet of the Urdu tradition.

> If the barman does not fill my cup soon,
> there will be cause for sorrow,
> because this hour of joy, this moment of
>   delight
> does not last, does not last, does not last,
>   does not last.
>
> (Zafar)

All of the following are couplets of Ghalib.

> The size of the cup is the only limit to
>   thirst.
> Were the ocean made of wine, I would be
>   a coastline, very long and very dry.
>
> One hundred times I have freed myself
>   from the chains of love.
> But how can I really escape when my own
>   heart is an enemy of freedom?
>
> Where, oh God, is desire's second step?
> In the wilderness of possibility, I have
>   found one foot print.
>
> I go a little way with every fast walker,
> Even so, I have yet to find a guide.
>
> From head to foot I am dedicated to love,
>   but how can I forget the love of my
>   existence?
> I worship the lightning, but regret its
>   effects.

I am not the bloom of song, nor the
intricate web of melody.
I am the sound of my own destruction.

His alone is sleep. His alone is peace of
mind.
His alone are the nights. Who has your
tresses spread out upon his arm.

European barbarism For almost a thousand years the civilization of Islam was probably the most sophisticated and prosperous in the world. As the following stories taken from the *Kitab al-Itibar*, a memoir written by a man named Usamah ibn Munqidh who lived in Palestine and died in 1199, show when Muslims first encountered Europeans, the Europeans were looked at as barbarians. The Franks, as all Europeans were known to Muslims, were thought of as ignorant and simple minded. This early experience of European barbarism may have hurt the Islamic world in the long run. When in the sixteenth and seventeenth centuries the nations of Europe became aggressive, the Muslim world did not take them seriously. This failure to recognize the threat had a hand in the Islamic world's inability to resist European control.

On the Medicine of the Franks

The Christian king of Al-Munaytirah
wrote to my uncle and asked him to send
a physician to treat some of his people
who were sick. My uncle sent him Thabit,
a physician who happened to be a
Christian. Thabit returned after only ten
days and we joked with him, saying "How
quickly you can heal your patients!" But
he told this story.

"They brought in a man who had a running sore on his leg. They also brought a woman who had gone mad. I placed a dressing filled with herbs on the wound and thus I tried to draw the infection out. As for the woman, I placed her on a diet in order to change her body humor by making it wet.[1]

"But while I was treating them, one of their own doctors, like them a Frank, came. 'This man is ignorant,' he said, pointing to me. 'He will never cure you.' He went up to the man who had the sore on his leg and said, 'Do you want to live with one leg or die with two?' The man said, 'I'd live with one.' The Frankish doctor then said, 'bring a strong knight with a sharp ax.' Soon the man appeared with the ax in his hands. While I (Thabit) was standing by looking on the Frankish physician put the patient's leg upon a block of wood. He told the axman, 'strike, take the leg off with a single blow.' So the man did strike, first one blow, but the leg was not taken off. Then he struck another blow. At this point the marrow in the leg began to flow and the man died at once. Then the Frankish doctor turned his attentions to the madwoman. He proclaimed, 'some demon has taken possession of this woman. Shave off the

---

[1]From the time of the Greeks it was believed that the four bodily "humors": phlegm, choler, black bile, and yellow bile controlled health. An imbalance in these humors, for instance an excess of "dry" humors, was thought to be the cause of diseases, in this case, the woman's madness. By changing the woman's diet, Thabit was trying to balance the humors. It sounds ridiculous to us, but for the time, it was very advanced.)

lady's hair.' So they did shave her head. The woman herself went off her diet and began eating garlic and mustard, things which the Franks customarily eat. Her madness returned and even increased. 'The demon has entered her skull,' said the Frankish doctor. At this he took a razor and made a deep cut in the form of a cross. He pulled back the skin so that the skull itself was exposed. Then he rubbed the wound with salt. The woman died immediately. As my services were no longer required, I returned here. I have learned something of the Frankish medicine that I had not known before."

Another Tale:
The Franks Have No Sense of Modesty

I heard a story from a man named Salim who was in charge of a public bath in one of the cities. He told how one day he opened the bath and found a Christian knight waiting for him. Now the Franks are very immodest. They will not wear a loin-cloth when they bathe. When this knight saw that Salim was wearing such a covering, he reached out and pulled it off him. It so happened that Salim had recently shaved off his pubic hair (an act of ritual purity for Muslims). When the knight saw that Salim was shaved below, he was amazed. He ran his hand over the place and said, "Salim, for God's sake do the same for me." He lay down on his back and Salim shaved off the knight's pubic hair, which was as thick as his beard. When the knight touched himself and felt the smoothness, he shouted,

"Salim, you must do this for my wife." So the knight sent his servant home to fetch his wife. When she arrived, the lady disrobed and lay on her back. While her husband looked on beaming, Salim shaved her. After this they thanked Salim and paid him. But, think of this contradiction! The Franks do not feel shame, nor do they feel jealousy, for they allow other men to gaze on their wives' nakedness, yet they are very brave. But how can they be brave? For courage is a product of zeal, ambition and the desire to be above reproach.

Glossary

Bedouin The Arab nomads of the desert.

Ibrahim, Musa, Isa Three of the many prophets who came before Muhammad. Ibrahim, known as Abraham in the Judeo-Christian tradition, was revered by both Jews and Muslims as their people's forefather. Musa was the Arabic form of the name Moses. Moses was famous as the liberator of the Jews from Egyptian bondage. Isa is the Arabic form of the name Jesus, whom the Muslims revere as a very great Prophet, but only as a Prophet.

Hadith (plural, Ahadith) Literally, "narration," these are the traditions that recount the sayings and doings of the Prophet. From the study of these anecdotes, Muslims seek to discover the *sunna,* the authoritative practice of the Prophet.

Khalifah Literally, "the successor," the term refers to those individuals who inherited Muhammad's temporal role of leader of the community of the faithful.

Khilafat The office of Khalifah, the institution of successorship.

Malik, Amir, Sultan Three different words used to refer to leaders called kings or princes in the European tradition. These leadership roles developed separately from the Khilafat and often flourished at the expense of central authority.

Madinah Literally, "the city," refers to the town north of Mecca to which Muhammad migrated in A.D. 622. Before the arrival of the Prophet it was known as Yathrib.

Mecca The city in the Arabian Peninsula in which Muhammad was born. Even before his time Mecca was a religious center for the Arabs. After Muhammad's success, Mecca became the religious center of the Islamic faith.

Hijra Literally, the "migration," Muhammad's move from Mecca to Madinah, which occurred in A.D. 622, but which is the first year of the Muslim calendar.

Quran Literally, "the reading," this is the written revelation of God (Allah) transmitted to Muhammad and gathered by his followers into a single book.

Shah Persian word translated as "king." The Iranian emperors were known as *Shahan Shah*: "The king of kings."

Shariah Literally, "the clear path," a word often badly translated as "Islamic law." It is the guideline, in theory, for the behavior of all good Muslims. It is, however, more a rule of conscience than what Euro-Americans think of as law.

Shiah Short for the Arabic phrase *Shiat ul-'Ali*, meaning the "party of Ali." This group held that only Ali, the Prophet's cousin and son-in-law, or his descendants were fit to lead the Muslim community. The Shiah sect is the minority sect in Islam, although it is strong in Iran, which has a Shiah majority and in the Gulf States where the Shiah are a numerically significant minority. (Do not confuse this with Shariah.)

Sunnah The authoritative example of the Prophet, established by his words and deeds and discovered through the study of the traditions (ahadith) about his life.

Surah A chapter of the *Quran*, for instance the *Fatihah*, the "opening" or first Surah of the *Quran*.

Sunni Short for the Arabic phrase, *Ahl al-sunnah wa Jamaat*: the people who follow the practice and are part of the community of the Prophet. This is the majority sect in Islam. Originally, it split with the Shiah over the issue of who would be *khalifah*. The Shiah asserted that only Ali or his descendants could hold the office. The Sunni held that any good Muslim could hold the position. Though it began as political division, over the years the two sects have developed some basic theological and ritualistic contradictions. Since the sixteenth century, the split between the two sects has created mutual antipathy and even provoked sectarian bloodshed.

"The People of the Book" The Muslim way of referring to Christians and Jews. These two groups were entitled to special protection since they each possessed, even in corrupted forms, books from God.

Ulama A word often inaccurately translated as "Islamic priesthood," or "Islamic clergy." There is no clergy in Islam. The root of the word comes from an Arabic term meaning knowledge (*ilm*). In this case, it is knowledge of the faith of Islam. Thus, the ulama are really a group of those learned in the faith. Its singular form is *alim*, one who has knowledge. Thus, the ulama are the body of those learned in the faith.

Ummah The body of believing Muslims. It is the "Community of Faith."

Suggestions for Further Reading

Arberry, A. J. *Aspects of Islamic Civilization.* Ann Arbor: U of Michigan P, 1978.

Asad, Muhammad. *The Road to Mecca.* London: Luzac, 1954.

Asad, T., ed. *Anthropology and the Colonial Encounter.* London: Cornell UP, 1973.

Boyle, John, ed. *Persian History and Heritage.* London: Henry Melland, 1969.

Breasted, James Henry. *Development of Religion and Thought in Ancient Egypt.* New York: Harper, 1959.

Ceram, C. W. *Gods, Graves and Scholars.* New York: Bantam, 1972.

Daniel, Norman. *Islam and the West: The Making of an Image.* Edinburgh: Edinburgh UP, 1960.

———. *Islam, Europe and Empire.* Edinburgh: Edinburgh UP, 1966.

Encyclopedia of Islam. 4 vols. 1st ed. Leiden: Brill, 1913-1942; 2nd ed. Leiden: Brill, 1960–.

Farmer, Edward, et al. *A Comparative History of Civilizations in Asia.* 2 vols. Boulder: Westview, 1985.

Fromkin, David. *A Peace to End All Peace.* New York: Avon, 1990.

Hodgson, Marshall. *The Venture of Islam.* 3 vols. Chicago: U of Chicago P, 1970.

Hourani, Albert. *A History of the Arab People.* Cambridge, MA: Belknap/Harvard, 1991.

Lewis Bernard, ed. *The Cambridge History of Islam.* 2 vols. Cambridge: Cambridge UP, 1970.

———. *Islam.* 2 vols. Oxford: Oxford UP, 1986.

Mertz, Barbara. *Red Land, Blackland.* New York: Dell, 1967.

Nesin, Aziz. *Istanbul Boy.* 2 vols. Austin: Middle East Studies Center, U of Texas, 1977–1979.

Olmstead, A. T. *History of the Persian Empire.* Chicago: U of Chicago P, 1970.

Peters, Francis E. *The Harvest of Hellenism: A History of the Near East From Alexander the Great to the Triumph of Christianity.* New York: Simon, 1978.

Pritchard, J. B., ed. *The Ancient Near East: An Anthology of Texts and Pictures.* 2 vols. Princeton: Princeton UP, 1962.

Rahman, Fazlur. *Islam.* 2nd ed. Chicago: U of Chicago P, 1979.

Robinson, Francis. *Atlas of the Islamic World since 1500.* New York: Facts on File, 1982.

Rodinson, Maxime. "The Western Image and Western Studies of Islam." *The Legacy of Islam.* Ed. J. Schacht. Oxford: Oxford UP, 1974.

Said, Edward. *Covering Islam: How the Media and the Experts Determine What We See of the Rest of the World.* New York: Pantheon, 1981.

———. *Orientalism.* New York: Random, 1979.

Voll, John. *Islam: Continuity and Change in the Modern World.* Boulder: Westview, 1982.

Bibliography

Barani, Zia ud-din. *Fatawa-i Jahandari*. Ed. A. S. Khan. Lahore: Anjaman-i taraqqi, 1972.

Barker, Muhammad Abd ur Rahman, et al., eds. *Naqsh-i Dilpazir: An Anthology of Classical Urdu Poetry*. 3 vols. Ithaca: Spoken Language Services, 1977.

Hodgson, Marshall. *The Venture of Islam*. 3 vols. Chicago: The U of Chicago P, 1974.

The Holy Bible. King James Version. New York: New American Library, 1974.

Khan, Baqir. *Mauizah-i Jahangiri*. Lahore: n.p., 1968.

The Koran Interpreted. Trans. Arthur J. Arberry. New York: Macmillan, 1974.

Kritzeck, J., ed. *Anthology of Islamic Literature*. New York: New American Library, 1964.

Lewis, B., ed. *Islam*. Vols. I and II, New York: Harper & Row, 1974.

Lewis, Bernard, ed. and trans. *Islam: From the Prophet Muhammad to the Capture of Constantinople*. New York: Harper, 1974.

ibn Munqidh, Usamah. *Kitab al-Itibar*. Ed. P. K. Hitti. Beirut: Libraire du Liban, 1950.

Sahih Muslim. Trans. A. H. Siddiqi. Lahore: Ashraf, 1973.

Sayings of Muhammad. Trans. G. Ahmad. Lahore: Ashraf, 1968.

The Zend-Avesta. Trans. J. Darmesteter. 3 vols. Oxford: Oxford UP, 1890. (As altered by Gregory C. Kozlowski.)